DIVORCE WISELY

MARRIAGES END.
FAMILIES DON'T.

DIVORCE WISELY.

The essential handbook for navigating the process of divorce

SUZANNE E. GRANDCHAMP, ESQ.

Copyright © 2015 Suzanne E. Grandchamp, Esq.
All rights reserved.

No part of this book may be reproduced, or stored in a retrieval system, or transmitted in any form or by any means, electronic, mechanical, photocopying, recording, or otherwise, without express written permission of the publisher.

Published by IngramSpark
ISBN-13 (paperback): 978-0-9964032-0-7
eISBN: 978-0-9964032-1-4

Cover design by Miladinka Milic (milagraphicartist.com)
Author photo by Matt Seefeldt (seefeldtphoto.com)
Edited by Lizzie Vance (knliterary.com)
Wheel of Life graphic on page 168, reprinted with permission by The Meyer Resource Group,® Inc.

Printed in the United States of America

Disclaimer: The information presented in this book is intended to provide the reader with *general* legal principles as well as information pertaining to the other aspects of divorce (emotional, financial, and personal growth). Please *do not* mistake any information provided herein for *legal advice* in the state in which you reside. Each state has its own set of laws with respect to divorce. While there is certainly some uniformity as to the legal principles involved in divorce, the author strongly suggests that the reader meet with a divorce attorney licensed to practice law in the state in which he or she resides in order to learn how the divorce laws in that state will apply to the reader's specific factual circumstances.

To all the people who are considering or going through the difficult transition of divorce — and who feel scared, lost, anxious, unsure of what comes next, or just plain terrified. This book was written for you, in the hopes that a *lot* of information about the process might make it a *little* easier.

Contents

Preface . . . xi

Introduction . . . 1

CHAPTER 1 **Are You Headed for Divorce? . . . 5**
Addressing the State of the Union
Should I Stay or Should I Go?
How Do You See Your Partner and Your Marriage?
Is There Willingness to Work on the Marriage?

CHAPTER 2 **Divorce 101: Processes and General Information . . . 13**
Is Divorce the Only Option Available?
Whose Fault Is It Anyway? Fault versus No-Fault
Divorce Readiness
Divorce Made Easier: Three General Rules to Play By
What Does the Divorce Process Look Like?
Who Chooses the Process and How Does the Process Begin?
What are the Summons and Petition?
Service of Process
Discovery: Getting Information Formally or Informally
How Long?
What Would Love Do?
Having the Hard Conversation

CHAPTER 3 **Hiring a (Good) Family Law Attorney . . . 47**
Do I Need an Attorney?
What if I Cannot Afford an Attorney?
How Do I Find a Good Attorney?

How Do I Know if the Attorney Is a "Good One" and Right for Me?
How Do I Pay for an Attorney's Services?

CHAPTER 4 **The Kids . . . 67**
Are My Kids Going to Be Okay if We Get Divorced?
When and How to Tell the Kids
What to Tell the Kids
Support and Nurture Your Children's Relationship
   with the Other Parent
Do Not Put Your Kids in the Middle
When Does the Child Get to Decide?

CHAPTER 5 **The Legal Divorce . . . 75**
Divorce Laws Vary by State
The Three *S*'s of Divorce
First *S*: Schedules
Second *S*: Support
Third *S*: Stuff

CHAPTER 6 **The Emotional Divorce . . . 113**
The Physiology of Emotions
Navigating the Pain
The Research on Gratitude
It's a Process: The Five Stages of Grief
Taking Blame out of the Equation
Keeping Your Emotional Balance during the Process of Divorce
Controlling the Controllable
Fighting as the Last Form of Intimacy
Domestic Abuse

CHAPTER 7 **The Financial Divorce . . . 135**
I'm Scared! I'm Not Familiar with Our Finances!
Knowledge (and Compiling Information!) is Power
Make Timely Payments and Keep Bills Current
What to Do with Joint Bank Accounts and Joint Credit Cards
Not All Assets Are Created Equal!
Basic Financial Management
Today Isn't Tomorrow: Cultivating and Planning
   for New Financial Dreams

CONTENTS

CHAPTER 8   **It's Over! Now What? ... 149**
Legal Clean-Up
Emotional Clean-Up

CHAPTER 9   **Divorce as an Opportunity for Growth and Transformation ... 159**
Reclaiming Your Personal Power and Creating Life Anew
Forgiveness
Dreaming New Dreams and Navigating Your Way to Them
Adult Attachment Theory: Knowing the Science Behind Attraction
How to Effectively Love and Feel Loved in a New Relationship:
   The Five Love Languages
Trusting Again After Divorce

Acknowledgments ... 179

APPENDIX A   Participation Agreement ... 181

APPENDIX B   Roadmap to Resolution ... 199

APPENDIX C   Erik Erikson's Developmental Stages ... 201

APPENDIX D   Balance Sheet ... 203

APPENDIX E   Cycle of Domestic Abuse ... 205

APPENDIX F   Budget Form ... 207

Notes ... 213

References ... 215

Preface

"What's up with the title of this book?" you may be asking. "How is it that marriages end, but families don't?" You may want to know what I mean by "divorcing wisely," and why you might want to consider doing so.

Fair enough! You may be surprised to learn that the title of this book relates to an important theoretical principle in physics, known as quantum entanglement.

Say what?

In 1982, a French physicist by the name of Alain Aspect conducted an experiment which demonstrated John Stewart Bell's theorem of inequality. The results of the experiment showed that particles, which have interacted and then been separated, are able to instantaneously communicate with each other, regardless of the physical distance between them. In other words, an event at one location can affect an event at another location, without any obvious mechanism for communication between the two locations. Albert Einstein was aware of this concept, and referred to it as "spooky action at a distance"!

"Thanks for the physics lesson, Suzanne, but how does this apply to me, my spouse, and our kids?" you might wonder. Here's how: you, your spouse, and your kids are "particles" that have interacted and then separated. Except, theoretically speaking, there really is no separation. Once you have interacted, you remain "entangled," even at a distance. In other words, what you do affects your spouse (and your kids), and vice versa, even if you two live across the country from each other. *Bazinga!*

So while it is true that marriages legally end, the bonds created during the marriage keep families connected forever. Intuitively, you know this. Just because you get a divorce doesn't mean you and your spouse stop raising your kids together. You will always have some connection, whether it be over your kids' schoolwork, at a basketball game, or later, at family weddings, graduations, and funerals. Even if you don't have kids together, the connection between spouses, and the impact one spouse has upon the other, are both profound and enduring.

Given this larger context, and considering how connected we *really* are (seemingly unbound by time and space), I suggest you give some serious thought as to how you're going to "show up," both during and after the transition called divorce. Are you going to be angry, nasty, retributive, controlling, manipulative, condescending, sarcastic, judgmental, and unforgiving? Or can you find the higher ground, and keep yourself primarily in a place of repose?

Finding that place of repose, albeit difficult at times, comes with a host of positive consequences. You'll feel better—physically and emotionally—throughout the divorce and beyond. You'll make informed, well-reasoned decisions, which reflect your values and your preferences, both for yourself and for your family. You'll feel good about yourself and your choices, regardless of your spouse's actions. And you'll be better prepared for your new life after the divorce is concluded.

So, that's what I mean by the title of this book. Marriages certainly end, but families don't. Divorce is simply a legal mechanism that *restructures* families. Instead of one family living under one roof, divorce essentially creates two roofs (with a bunch of legal obligations between them) for one family. Like most things in life, this transition can be done well, or it can be done poorly. You can choose to do it well. You can choose to *divorce wisely*.

Introduction

Divorce is right up there as one of the most difficult transitions in life—right next to death, a scary health diagnosis, or another traumatic disruption in life, like the loss of a job. Divorce is a time of being overwhelmed. It is a time of feeling afraid and uncertain of the future. It is a time when the world is turned upside down and everything looks strangely distorted and out of place.

Whether you're in the middle of divorce, or are just contemplating the prospect, the process can be daunting. This book aims to make both the process, and the information you need to make the best decisions for you and your future, easily accessible.

This book's organization is straightforward. The first topic covered deals with assessing whether or not your marriage is salvageable. This is not a subject I learned in law school, and most divorce lawyers won't be able to educate you about this. Truly though, it's where you may want to begin if you're not sure about what's next. Perhaps surprisingly, the key elements to a healthy, functional marriage are no secret, but neither are the signs of a deeply troubled marriage. I'll talk through all this with you in chapter 1.

If you've decided that the marriage is not salvageable, then the next step is to assess the various options available to you, as well as how to hire and work with a good family law attorney. If you're headed for divorce, we'll talk about how you can best support your kids through this difficult transition. We'll also take the fear out of the legalities of the divorce and treat it as a business transaction that can be broken down into three aspects.

The much larger component of the divorce is the emotional roller coaster of releasing and grieving the marriage relationship. We'll talk about strategies for keeping your sanity intact during this crazy process.

We'll also talk about a host of issues that relate to the financial aspect of divorce. You'll learn how to safeguard yourself financially, whether you're intimately familiar with your family's finances or have never balanced your check book.

And as we near the end of the book, we'll walk through the finalization of the whole legal process, and we'll discuss how to navigate the multitudes of endings and new beginnings. Divorce is a prime opportunity for your personal growth and transformation, so as we wrap up, we'll talk about how postdivorce is a time for setting new boundaries and dreaming new dreams. It's also a time that can offer much in the way of learning about yourself, and many opportunities for the practices of forgiveness and trust.

I envisioned, wrote, and organized this book so that you could pick it up at any point and turn to exactly what you need in that moment. It can then be set down and picked up at any other point when you need to learn about, or reference, another topic. Or, maybe you will read it cover to cover one evening as you lay awake, unable to sleep. You will do whatever is right for you, and you have easy access to what you need to know, exactly when you need to know it.

Before we proceed, a suggestion: be good to yourself during this time. And be gentle. This is a traumatic transition, even if you and your spouse are amicable and in agreement on everything. Divorce involves a lot of releasing (think of all of the hopes and dreams you had about your marriage) and a lot of surrendering (because you don't one-sidedly control the process). Release and surrender are rarely easy. They are usually circuitous, often unwieldy, and they always take time.

Give yourself the time to release and to mourn. So often, I see people who attempt to avoid the pain of divorce by circumventing it through the fleeting pleasure of a new relationship. Ultimately, however, there is no way around the pain—there is only making your way through it. Avoided pain tends to compound substantial interest, just like high interest rate credit cards. Feeling the pain, though uncomfortable at times, will move you more quickly through the difficult emotions that accompany divorce.

If you have minor children, you'll also be helping them through the process. Please remember that you can't give them what you don't have. So, just like in the event of an airplane emergency, you first put the oxygen mask on yourself, and then your child.

Also remember that you are modeling behavior for your children to emulate throughout this transition. What would you have them see—kindness, empathy, compassion, forgiveness, strength, and courage? Or something else? No matter how mad you may be, the studies about kids and divorce are clear: kids do better if their parents do not put them into the middle of a bitter or spiteful divorce. Bottom line: love your kids more than you hate your spouse.

You're going to get through this, and I'm going to help by giving you the general information you need to begin thinking about what's best for you and your family. Because divorce laws vary by state, it is important to use this book as a *starting point* for gathering information about the process. You will also need to learn more about the specific divorce laws in your home state.

So, with that, let's get started.

Are You Headed for Divorce?

Addressing the State of the Union

Not everyone who comes into my office is destined for divorce. In fact, many people make an initial consultation to learn more about the process so that they can decide between whether to divorce or to stay in the marriage.

What I've learned over the years is that most people don't understand what makes a marriage work or what the signs are of a deeply troubled marriage. I know I didn't! Only after some time giving divorce presentations with an insightful divorce coach did I pick up the essentials of what makes a happy marriage and how to spot the warning signs of divorce.

As it turns out, neither the ingredients to a successful marriage nor the signs of a troubled marriage are secrets. There has been research conducted on thousands of couples over several decades that has left little to doubt when it comes to what creates a happy, mutually satisfying marriage.

The person responsible for considerable research in this area is a man by the name of Dr. John Gottman. Dr. Gottman is a professor emeritus at the University of Washington in Seattle and has been studying marriage—and couples—for over forty years in both his Love Lab at the university and through his work at The Gottman Institute.[1]

After much research and analysis, Dr. Gottman found that there was not one type of marriage that was more, or less, predictive of success. Here are the three different styles of problem solving into which marriages can be grouped: 1) validating, 2) volatile, and 3) conflict avoiding.

Couples who fall into the validating subgroup compromise often and calmly work out their problems to mutual satisfaction as they arise. In the volatile style, conflict erupts frequently, resulting in passionate disputes. And couples who fall into the conflict-avoiding style tend to agree to disagree, and do not generally confront their differences.

Prior to Dr. Gottman's research, many psychologists considered conflict avoiding and volatile marriages to be destructive. But after studying these relationships for decades, Dr. Gottman considers all three styles to be equally stable and to bode equally well for the marriage's longevity.

So, if there's not a type of marriage that predicts success, then what does? Interestingly, Dr. Gottman did find one attribute that highly correlates to a successful marriage. This attribute is the balance between the amounts of positivity and negativity in the marriage. By *balance*, Gottman does not mean *equal* amounts of positivity and negativity. By carefully studying the amount of time couples spent fighting versus interacting positively, like touching, smiling, paying compliments, or laughing, Gottman and his team came up with a very specific ratio between the amount of positivity and negativity that exists in a stable marriage. This ratio is five to one, meaning there have to be five positive interactions to every negative one. In other words, in order for a marriage to be stable over time, it has to be 80 percent positive and only 20 percent negative.

The couples in Dr. Gottman's Love Lab who were headed for divorce were doing too little—as far as positively engaging with each other—to make up for the growing negativity between them. Dr. Gottman also found that the same growing negativity in these relationships had obvious—and predictable—earmarks and flags. Some of these flags include:

- a harsh startup (think starting an argument with sarcasm, accusations, or criticism);

- flooding (when a spouse's negativity is so overwhelming and sudden that it leaves the other spouse feeling defenseless and shell-shocked);

- closed-off body language;

- ignored or failed attempts to repair an argument;

- negatively rewriting marital memories;

- and lastly, something Gottman calls the four horsemen.

Just as the four horsemen signal the apocalypse in Christianity, Gottman named the four following traits the four horsemen, as they are reliable indicators of a marital apocalypse. The first of the horsemen is blame, the second is defensiveness, the third is contempt, and the fourth is stonewalling.

The horsemen are disastrous ways of interacting that sabotage communication between partners, thereby lessening intimacy and trust. Once these negative ways of interacting make regular appearances in the marriage, a snowball effect occurs, with one or both partners increasing their focus on the negativity and tension within the marriage. The horsemen also have a collective energy, and they build upon each other, insidiously overtaking the marriage.

HORSEMAN #1: CRITICISM

Criticism is an attack on someone's personality or character—usually with blame—assigning them the responsibility for the wrong. This is different from a complaint, which focuses on a behavior.

Often, criticisms are generalizations. They appear in statements like "you always" or "you never." For example, a criticism of your spouse's failure to take out the garbage might sound like this: "Apparently, the garbage empties itself in your world. You are so lazy; you never see what needs to be done around here. It pisses me off." Here, the criticism attacks the spouse's character, describing them as lazy, and adds the generalization that they "never" see what needs to be done.

On the flip side, a complaint would be more along these lines: "I noticed you didn't take the garbage out again this week. It seems like this is a pattern, and that really bothers me." The emphasis in the latter is on the task not being done rather than on belittling or degrading the character of the person. The continual criticism of someone's personality and/or character builds up resentments. These resentments, in turn, make way for the second horseman: contempt.

HORSEMAN #2: CONTEMPT

Dr. Gottman describes contempt as "lobbing insults into the heart of your partner's sense of self."[2] Contempt takes criticism and dials it up several notches. As I see it, criticism is a put-down of the partner, born of frustration. Contempt is the *intention* to insult and psychologically abuse the partner. It comes in the form of hostile humor, mockery, and body language (think eye rolling, sneering, and so on). When contempt has poisoned the relationship, it is hard to remember any positive qualities, attributes, or acts of the partner. And when respect leaves the relationship, the path is paved for the last two horsemen: defensiveness and stonewalling.

HORSEMAN #3: DEFENSIVENESS

Defensiveness plays out when neither partner takes responsibility for setting things right. It can be summed up as "It's not me, it's *you*!" It shows up as denying responsibility, making excuses, repeating yourself and your position (as opposed to trying to understand your partner), and cross-complaining (answering a complaint with a complaint). This pattern of consistent interaction continues to toxify the relationship to the point where the partners just don't care anymore. And this leads to the fourth and final horseman: stonewalling.

HORSEMAN #4: STONEWALLING

The consistent appearance of this fourth and final horseman signals the end of caring enough to communicate at all, and is often the death knell of the relationship. Gottman says the marriage goes from "being marred by poor communication to being virtually destroyed by [no communication]."[3]

A stonewaller simply checks out. They mumble "uh-huh" or "mm-hmm" as responses to their spouse's statements or questions. Maybe the stonewaller hides behind a newspaper, iPad, or iPod, and is silent in reaction to a question or comment by his or her spouse. Regardless, the action (or better, *in*action) conveys an air of disapproval, iciness, or smugness.

Gottman notes that women, in particular, are especially irritated by stonewalling. These women don't feel loved, heard, seen, or acknowledged. Perhaps this horseman is particularly annoying to women because we live in a society that has historically devalued women's opinions and worth. That said, I will tell you that I have had plenty of male clients who have been steamed by their spouse's stonewalling. These male clients have also felt disrespected, devalued, and marginalized.

Take heart: evidence of one or more of the horsemen is not *necessarily* the end of the marriage. The consistent expression of *all* the horsemen, though, signals a severing of the marital bonds, through deeply embedded negativity that predictably destroys relationships.

Should I Stay or Should I Go?

So, maybe your marriage occasionally has harsh start-ups, flooding, or failed repair attempts. Maybe one or more of the horsemen occasionally make an appearance during an argument or at the breakfast table. Now what? Do you hang up the marriage or try to work through the issues?

In my experience, this is a deeply personal question for everyone. There is no one right answer. In almost twenty years of practice, however, I have noticed some important—albeit anecdotal—markers that I will share with you. And in the interest of transparency, I want to be clear that my own observations echo much of Dr. Gottman's research.

How Do You See Your Partner and Your Marriage?

Over the course of the last two decades, I have learned to look for how my prospective client talks about his or her spouse, as well as the general state of the marriage. I know there is deep distress when my prospective client refers to the spouse and/or the marriage in a wholly negative light. If there is no positive regard left for the spouse, this clues me in on the fact that the relationship *is* deeply troubled. Often, I will ask the client to name two or three positive attributes about their spouse. You might be surprised to learn that many can think of none, or only one or two, when posed with this question. In my experience, not having space left for positive regard is a huge red flag that the marriage is in serious trouble. My anecdotal experience mirrors Dr. Gottman's research. He has found that marriages are in danger when one (or both) of the spouses sees their marriage problems as severe. Couples who have repetitive, pervasive, negative thoughts about their marriages, and who interact poorly with each other (think the four horsemen, the unwillingness of one—or both—to accept influence from each other, harshness and lack of admiration or appreciation of each other, and the like), have unhealthy marriages.

Is There Willingness to Work on the Marriage?

How willing are you to work on your marriage? How willing is your spouse to work on the marriage? Are each of you willing to attend and actively participate in therapy? Are you two willing to re-allot energy and resources away from your kids, your jobs, and your friends and relatives to make the time to repair the relationship? Do both of you think it's possible to repair the damage?

In Dr. Gottman's experience and my own, couples who are on the edge of divorce are often unwilling to commit the time and resources to repair the marriage. Instead, they begin to lead parallel, but separate, lives. She goes out with only her friends to decompress and have fun. He travels exclusively with his buddies and socializes with his work colleagues. When this shift happens, the couple stops talking things over. It seems useless. Each begins to problem-solve joint issues—like the kids or the finances—on his or her own, without input from the other spouse.

To be sure, this stage of "parallel but separate" leads to loneliness within the marriage. Often, one or both partners may have an affair to quell the loneliness. Gottman sees an affair as a symptom of a dying marriage, not the cause. And I would agree. Usually, when I meet with a prospective client, the "affair"—either theirs or their spouse's—is the proverbial last straw, ending a marriage that had been mortally wounded for a long time.

If you and your spouse, however, decide to work on the marriage, the importance of focusing on what's positive can't be overemphasized. To recap, Gottman cracked the code to saving marriages, and it came from his analysis of *what went right* in happy marriages. The keys to righting a troubled marriage come from how a couple interacts when they're *not* fighting—not how they handle their disagreements.

In short, it is often the case that couples go on living separate, dissatisfied lives and marriages because they haven't been willing to do what this chapter suggests: address the state of the union.

If you're willing to do this, the review can be either hope filled or sobering . . . and often it is both. If you're on the precipice of really evaluating your marriage's health and haven't done so yet, ask yourself the following questions.

- Can I honestly say that I am happy in my marriage?

- Do I know if my spouse is happy in our marriage?

- Do either my spouse or I engage, regularly, in any of the four horsemen behaviors?

- Does one (or both) of us see the marriage as mostly negative?

- Do we lead parallel but separate lives? If so, is each of us willing to let go of some of this in order to have a more unified marriage?

- Are both of us willing to work on the marriage?

There are no right or wrong answers to these questions. Discerning both partners' feelings about their engagement in the marriage often can lead to a whole new set of awarenesses and decisions to make. You may decide that you're willing to give it another go, and if that's the case, you have my blessing.

If on the other hand, you've given all you can, and you are clear that your marriage is over, I can provide information and tools which will help you move through this transition.

Divorce 101: Processes and General Information

So, you think you may be headed for divorce. Or perhaps, your spouse has decided this. Maybe you were just served with court papers. You have a knot in your stomach the size of a basketball, and it makes you feel sick. What now? What next?

First, breathe! You're not going to do anyone any good—most importantly, yourself—if you stop breathing, pass out, and collapse into unconsciousness! And remember, this too shall pass. All of these feelings will one day be a distant memory. You will make it through, and I am going to help by giving you information—lots of it! My goal in all of this is for you to be fully informed in going through this process. I want you to clearly understand the options available to you, so that you may choose wisely from among them. Information is power, as the saying goes, but it also has a calming effect, in my experience. To paraphrase the late Maya Angelou, when you know better, you can do better. And I would add, feel better, too! So, with that, let's get started!

Is Divorce the Only Option Available?

When I meet with someone for the first time, they're usually in a state of turmoil. They don't know what their options are or which way to go.

Many are surprised to learn that divorce is not the only legal option. Let's talk about the different legal options available to you, and also about annulment, which many clients wonder about as well.

Divorce is a legal process that extinguishes the bonds of matrimony between a legally married couple. Not only does it sever the marital relationship between you and your spouse, but divorce may also create ongoing legal obligations (think parenting, child support, and maintenance/alimony) between you, if applicable.

There is a finality about divorce. You will no longer be married. You will mostly lead separate lives (even if you have children together), and the decisions you make about your life will not generally affect your former spouse and vice versa. Your loyalties will shift. You will confide in other people, and be supported by your friends, relatives, and perhaps a new partner. Even if you have kids together, the coparenting relationship won't look like a marriage. Most often, it will look like a business arrangement that revolves around the kids' schedules.

Unlike a divorce, a legal separation does not extinguish the bonds of matrimony. While your marital relationship may still be legally intact, a legal separation looks a lot like divorce otherwise. Most spouses do not live together. They have legal documents that outline who parents the kids when, who pays whom child support and/or maintenance/alimony, as well as who gets what as far as property on an interim basis. A legal separation may not permanently divide up property, and you may still acquire marital assets and liabilities after the legal separation has been filed with the court. This varies by state, so if you're considering a legal separation, you need to know how your state handles the issue of property that is acquired after the legal separation.

I can count on one hand, the number of legal separations I have helped clients obtain over my nineteen years of practice. Why so few? Most cases that start out as a legal separation end in divorce. This is because if one spouse would prefer to be divorced, as opposed to being legally separated, a divorce proceeding usually "trumps" a legal separation proceeding. And many people are quite leery of having any possible lingering financial connections to their spouses, especially with regard to the acquisition of assets and debts after the legal separation.

I mean, how would you feel if your spouse amassed $40,000 in gambling debts on a credit card, which was ultimately deemed a marital debt at a later date? Most people choose not to live with this anxiety and opt, instead, for divorce.

In addition to legal separation and divorce, there is generally a process to end a marriage that was entered by a party who lacked the capacity to consent to the marriage, either because the person was underage, mentally infirm, under the influence of a mood-altering substance, or (ahem!) had a sexual incapacity that prevented the consummation of the marriage. When this occurs, you can bring a proceeding to have the court declare the marriage null and void. Some states refer to this as an annulment, which is not the same as a religious decree. In many states, this is referred to as a voidable marriage.

In addition to voidable marriages, there are void marriages, which really aren't marriages at all. You don't need to bring a proceeding to have them declared as void, because they really never existed in the first place. These types of unions include "marriages" between siblings, parent and child, people who are legally married to other people, and sometimes people who are developmentally disabled.

Over the course of my career, I have had very few encounters with void or voidable marriages. In chatting with my colleagues, their experiences seem to mirror my own. I attribute this to the fact that most people date, usually for a significant period of time prior to getting married, and know enough about their spouses not to end up with a void or voidable marriage. I also believe that most people actually think pretty seriously about getting married before solemnizing the relationship legally. I can honestly say that I've never had a client who got hitched in Vegas, while intoxicated, and who wanted a divorce shortly thereafter. So, maybe it is true that what happens in Vegas tends to stay in Vegas!

Many people want to know if their marriage can simply be annulled. These clients often come from a religious perspective, and see the marriage as never actually having existed, due to a lack of commitment on their spouse's part. The annulment they're seeking, however, is generally not a legal construct (even though some states use the word *annulment* to describe the legal process used to extinguish a voidable marriage). Rather, an annulment is something you may want to pursue within your own religious organization if this idea appeals to you. For example, I have had Catholic clients who have pursued a religious annulment after the divorce was legally finalized, because they wanted to be able to marry again within the Catholic Church.

Whose Fault Is It Anyway? Fault Versus No-Fault

Is the divorce someone's fault legally? Will either my spouse or I be held legally responsible for the demise of our marriage and the resulting divorce? If so, what does this mean, as far as the divorce goes? Could either of us be penalized for having caused the divorce?

The answer is . . . it depends.

Many states have done away with fault finding when it comes to divorce. These states are known as *no-fault jurisdictions*. This means that neither party will be deemed at fault for the breakdown of the marital relationship. The court will not spend any time determining who is responsible for the demise of the marriage. Rather, the court will accept the assertion of one party or both parties, in the initial court paperwork, that the marriage has had an "irretrievable breakdown," or that the parties have "irreconcilable differences," without any sort of offer of proof.

Some states, however, have a fault-based approach incorporated into their divorce laws. Certain states even have the option of pursuing a no-fault divorce or a fault-based divorce (for example Ohio, Indiana, and New York). In these states, the issue of fault may come into play and, if proved, may have an impact on either the allocation of assets and liabilities or an award (or lack thereof) of spousal support (alimony).

In states that offer both no-fault and fault-based processes, many couples select the no-fault approach. Why? The belief is that the no-fault option leads to a quicker overall resolution to the divorce than a fault-based approach. A fault-based divorce often takes more time, because the issue of fault has to be determined, as well as how it affects the other issues in the divorce (such as spousal support or property allocation). As you can imagine, the discussions and hearings regarding the issue of fault may be heated and protracted, and could result in a longer and more costly divorce. This may appeal to some people, especially if they feel betrayed or otherwise wronged by their partner during the marriage. Others just want to be done, and choose to bypass fault finding entirely in favor of finality and closure.

Whether your state is no-fault, fault based, or has both options, is something you can learn from an initial consultation with a divorce attorney licensed to practice law in the state in which you reside. Otherwise, you can research this issue yourself and determine your state's preference for fault finding in the context of divorce.

Divorce Readiness

Divorce readiness (meaning each partner's perspective on, and willingness to go through with, the divorce) is a topic that comes up in every case. Sometimes, both parties know the marriage is over, and just want to get done. Both may work together to collect information, fill out forms, or file legal paperwork to get through the process as quickly and easily as possible. It may be the case that you don't want to be divorced or maybe you're ready to be divorced today. Perhaps your spouse just learned that you wanted a divorce, and has pressed the "Ignore" button. Or maybe your spouse agrees that the marriage is over, and promises to meet with a divorce attorney to get information about the process. But it has been six weeks, and your spouse has not yet scheduled an appointment. Any of this sound familiar?

Ideally, you and your spouse would have the same divorce readiness. Both would agree that the marriage is over, and the process of coming to terms with respect to the kids, the money, and the property of the marriage would be straightforward. This does happen, but I would say that it tends to be more the exception than the rule. More often than not, one person wants to be divorced (and the quicker the better!), while the other spouse isn't quite ready for the transition.

What you need to know about the difference between partners, as far as divorce readiness goes, is that it can be very frustrating for each spouse! The partner who wants to be divorced yesterday doesn't understand why everything is taking so dang long! The partner who is not yet ready to be divorced doesn't understand why everything seems to be moving so dang quickly! The partner who wants to be divorced immediately gets an opportunity to practice patience. The partner who does not want to be divorced (or as quickly) often needs therapy, coaching, or simply time to work through some of the emotional issues related to divorce.

In addition, it may be helpful for both parties to participate in what's commonly known as *closure therapy*. In this type of therapy, you and your spouse participate together in a few therapy sessions with an accredited therapist, not for the purposes of trying to save the marriage, but to enhance your communication skills to work through some of the divorce-related emotions. This can be an especially useful tool if there are lingering resentments from either the marriage itself, or the way in which it ended, and you have minor children who will need to be coparented after the legal divorce is concluded. It can also help the two of you get through the divorce process more easily. To this end, there are three rules that I suggest my clients live by during the process of divorce.

Divorce Made Easier: Three General Rules to Play By

Divorce is often a painful transition, regardless of whether it's amicable or not. But to be sure, there are three rules to live by during the process of divorce that can help lessen the difficult feelings.

1. Get outside help.

2. Get a dog, not a boyfriend/girlfriend.

3. Don't be a jerk. Period.

Allow me to explain each in detail.

RULE #1 – GET OUTSIDE HELP

No matter how much your family and friends love you, they will become saturated and overwhelmed if you share every twist and turn of your journey through Divorceland with them. Don't do it.

That said, of course it is important to share your experience with your family and friends, but give them the Cliff's Notes version of what is going on, not the 585-page, blow-by-blow, serial novel.

It is also perfectly acceptable (and important) to ask for, and receive, their support during this time. But recognize the inherent limitations in support from family and friends.

First, most people going through divorce do not have family or friends who are trained psychologists or divorce coaches. So, their perspectives are going to be limited to supporting you through the subjective experience of divorce—not providing a broader context of divorce as a process that has physical, emotional, intellectual, and spiritual components.

Additionally, your friends and family cannot, and should not, be objective about your divorce. Their only job is to love you. You are the home team, and your family and friends should be sitting in your bleachers, wearing your colors, and rooting for you.

You do, however, need objective feedback about what you're going through and what is ahead of you. Objective feedback is information and perspective provided by a trained professional, like a psychologist or a divorce coach. Why do you need their input?

Two reasons.

First, knowledge is power. There is a lot of psychological "stuff" that gets played out in divorce. It can be very helpful for the parties to learn about this "stuff." It provides both an understanding of, and a context for, the experience. Invariably, clients who work with an objective professional end up feeling more secure when they discover what's going on below the surface, which helps lessen their internal fears and discomfort.

Second, the objective professional will also help you question and process your assumptions and expectations about divorce. This is invaluable because, believe it or not, you may actually have some misperceptions about your marriage, your spouse, the law, the process of divorce, or perhaps the world in general. Really! It is much more helpful, and cost-effective, for you to work through these projections in a therapeutic context, as opposed to spending tens of thousands of dollars working through them in the legal process.

RULE #2 – GET A DOG, NOT A BOYFRIEND/GIRLFRIEND

Love is good! Starting a new intimate relationship while getting divorced is not. Don't get the love you need by finding a new squeeze while going through divorce. Instead, get a dog. The dog will love you unconditionally during this process and beyond. Furthermore, dog food and vet bills are far cheaper than the expenses associated with dating!

As I mentioned earlier, there is a lot of psychological "stuff" going on during divorce. Take time to learn about this "stuff" and to process it. There is no shortcut to feeling the sadness, grief, or anger that always accompany divorce. You can try and avoid these feelings, as well ditch the opportunity to learn about yourself so you don't make the same mistakes in the future, by immersing yourself in the busyness and the feel-good pheromones that come with a new relationship.

Make no mistake, however. The sadness, grief, and anger will eventually catch up with you. When they come a-callin', they will surface at the most inopportune time (like in a fight with your new squeeze). What a mess! Then you will be dealing with the old feelings in the new relationship, and that is like mixing oil and water. Good luck!

Also, divorce is the best opportunity out there for you to take the time to learn about what went wrong, and how you contributed to both the successes and the failures of the marriage. Focus on yourself and on meeting your own needs. If you are not yet strong enough to support yourself with your own self-love, then get a dog. You will get the love and companionship you crave, without all of the baggage that comes with a new relationship started during a divorce.

This is not to say that dating is off limits forever. Once you are through the divorce, and if you have been doing your work, which I see as healing and learning from the loss of your marriage, you will be ready to date *after* your divorce is finished. If you have any question as to whether you are ready, get the input of your therapist or coach.

RULE #3 – DON'T BE A JERK. PERIOD.
This is, by far, the hardest rule to follow throughout the divorce.

Regardless of how amicable, or not, your divorce is, you will be tested—in multiple ways and often. In response, you will either decide to respond from a place of integrity or not.

By definition, *integrity* means the quality of being honest and having strong moral principles. This definition is not quite complete, because integrity also means the state of being whole and undivided. When you knit the two definitions together, integrity means you are going to act in a principled way from the parts of you that are whole and undivided, as opposed to acting in a dishonorable fashion from the parts of you that feel less-than and divided.

Bottom line: you will have to make a choice—at each and every turn. Some of these decisions may be easy, like figuring out who will get the Tupperware. Some of these decisions may be extraordinarily difficult, like figuring out when each of you will see your kids or determining the length and duration of spousal maintenance. In these moments—the easy and the difficult—you will need to decide who you are. Are you going to act from the best parts of you or the worst? Are you going to be kind or spiteful? Are you going to be honest or lie? I suggest you choose integrity—and for good reason.

In divorce, one factor, and one factor alone, is responsible for screwing up kids and driving the length and the cost of the proceeding through the roof. This factor is the level of acrimony between the parties. The greater the animosity between you and your spouse, the worse your kids fair, and the more money you and your spouse will spend on attorneys, child psychologists, and court costs. And the crappier you will feel when all is said and done.

Inasmuch as you might like to, you cannot control how your spouse acts during the divorce. Instead of trying to make your spouse behave, I advise you to control the controllable, which is you and your response. Even if your spouse is a complete jerk throughout the divorce, the acrimony will be one-half of what it otherwise would have been by your refusal to engage your spouse in the endless game of tit for tat, jib for jab, strike and parry.

I guarantee you will be happier with this approach, as will your children. And while you need not really care about how your spouse responds, in my experience some spouses are torqued by my clients' refusal to engage (which often makes my clients very happy), while other spouses begin to see the futility of getting their needs met through hostility, and magically their tone softens.

Standing in integrity and refusing to engage your spouse does not mean being a pushover in the divorce. Far from it. In fact, I believe "no" is a complete sentence, which needs neither an explanation nor a justification. She wants you to parent the kids three days a month only? No. He wants you to live on $500 per month when your marital standard of living was $5,000 per month? No. Get comfortable with this one-word answer, and with the other one-word answer ("yes"), and leave the defense of your interests to your attorney.

What Does the Divorce Process Look Like?

In my experience, most people who are considering divorce have many of the same questions. Everyone wants to know what the process looks like: How does it begin? Do we have to go to court? How long is it going to take? How much is it going to cost, and do I need a lawyer? Let's take these questions one by one.

Regardless of where you live, the process of divorce is fairly uniform. And for the sake of formality and comfort, instead of always using the term *parties*, as the legal documents would, I'm going to make this personal and address you, the reader, even if your only involvement is supporting someone who is going through this process.

So to begin, either you or your spouse will take that first step toward finding out about divorce and gathering information. Part of the basic information involves learning about the processes available to resolve whatever outstanding issues may be part and parcel of your divorce, like custody, parenting time, child support, and so forth.

Following are seven processes that are generally available to divorcing couples. I have arranged them from the *least* amount of intervention from a third party (like a mediator or the court) to the *most* amount of intervention.

1. The "Kitchen Table" Approach
2. Negotiation
3. Mediation
4. Cooperative Law
5. Collaborative Law
6. Arbitration
7. Litigation

Least Intervention — Most Intervention

THE "KITCHEN TABLE" APPROACH

This method is for those couples who can literally sit around the kitchen table and discuss and resolve the issues relevant to their divorce. They can agree on who should parent the kids when, as well as how to share their money and divide up the assets. When I share this method with my prospective clients, many of them laugh out loud and say, "If we could get along this well, we wouldn't be divorcing!"

Regardless, many couples realize that they are in the best position to resolve their issues, and that they can save *a lot* of money by choosing to be amicable and talking things out themselves. This is actually possible! Despite what you might see in the media about high-profile, high-conflict celebrity divorces, many divorcing couples do not have either highly contentious or highly complex issues. So, why pay someone to figure out solutions to relatively straightforward concerns? To this end, some states and many private companies offer online, do-it-yourself legal paperwork designed to help couples, with straightforward divorces, complete and file the forms on their own.

A fair number of divorcing couples, however, do have contested or complex issues. And, as you might imagine, many couples simply cannot get along well enough to work out the issues by themselves. When it's impossible to work things out on your own, you have many options to help you achieve a final, global resolution to your outstanding issues.

With the exception of Collaborative Law, all the other processes can be undertaken with or without an attorney. Whether you should do so is a question we will discuss in greater detail in the next chapter.

NEGOTIATION

In negotiation, you and your spouse engage in give-and-take discussions (verbally or in writing) in an effort to try and reach resolution. This communication can take place directly between you and your spouse or through attorneys. Negotiation often involves compromises on both sides in exchange for gains made on the issues most important to each of you. Negotiation can take place at any point in the process. Generally, the sooner it occurs in the process, the more quickly (and less expensively) the case can be resolved.

That said, effective negotiation can really only happen after you have openly exchanged information about all of the issues that are part of the divorce—which is called the *discovery phase*. If discovery doesn't happen, negotiation occurs in the blind, which may not be seen as fair to the courts. As property settlements tend to be final once reduced to writing and signed, it is best to make sure you have knowledge about everything that's out there *before* you start negotiating trades and making compromises.

COOPERATIVE LAW VS. COLLABORATIVE LAW

Though the processes of cooperative law and Collaborative Law are similar, their differences are important. In cooperative law, you and/or your attorneys work *together* toward mutually agreeable resolutions to each of the outstanding issues. Often, neutral experts (if they're needed) are used, like a real estate appraiser, and both sides will informally exchange information (*informal discovery*) before discussing settlement options. If, however, either side feels they need more direction or support, they can file the case with the court or seek court intervention at any time.

Although the idea of intervention might seem intimidating, it can help keep the divorce train on the tracks and chugging toward resolution. This is because you both know that a judge will be checking in on and managing the process. In other words, involving the court can provide a structured format and timeline to assist you and your spouse with the overwhelming and seemingly insurmountable task of untangling your lives.

In contrast to cooperative law, Collaborative Law involves the signing of a participation agreement (see appendix A) which states that your collaborative attorneys agree *not* to go to court for assistance or intervention. If either of you decides to involve the court for direction (other than to finalize your divorce), then you both must fire your Collaborative Law attorneys and hire new attorneys who can litigate your cases and represent you in court.

At first blush, this might seem harsh. Who wants to hire new attorneys if the process isn't working? Some attorneys and parties don't like this requirement, and won't use the process for this reason. Collaborative attorneys, however, claim that the vast majority of cases stay in the collaborative process, and very few need to opt out and proceed to court. This may be because both parties understand that the Collaborative Law path will likely yield more cooperation and less financial burden than proceeding to court. The "opportunity cost" of moving on to litigation, and choosing to start over, is intended to keep couples invested in the Collaborative Law approach when difficulties arise during the process.

In my experience with Collaborative Law (which, by the way, is the process I prefer if the case is appropriate), the cases almost always stay in the process. Why? I believe it is because the couples are often more emotionally ready for divorce, and tend to be less adversarial. Collaborative Law participants usually value taking the "high road" and maintaining a cordial, postdecree parenting relationship, and thus choose a process that promotes respect, civility, and transparency in the process of becoming divorced.

As a part of the Collaborative Law process, each of you must be represented by your own attorney. You, your spouse, and your respective attorneys will all meet together and work through a process that Collaborative Law aptly calls the *roadmap to resolution* (see appendix B). The roadmap to resolution sets forth the steps to follow before negotiating, and ultimately resolving, the divorce.

Often as a part of this process, neutral "team members" are involved to help each of you understand and work through issues. Most commonly, these team members include financial neutrals (who can help you sort out your assets and liabilities as well as create cash flow analyses, which help both sides understand your income and spending patterns) and child specialists (who help you and your spouse map out parenting time schedules and responsibilities). It is also helpful for both parties to work with an accredited mental health provider to help process the emotions of divorce and enhance communication skills. This can be extremely valuable, especially when there are unstated and unresolved emotional issues that may be frustrating the collaborative process and delaying resolution.

One of the main benefits of either cooperative law or Collaborative Law is that, if they successfully resolve the case, there is often no need for either of you, your children, or even your lawyers to set foot into court. The paperwork can usually be sent in by mail or filed electronically.

Sometimes, however, you may need outside input to help reach resolution or move you through an impasse. When this happens, you can use mediation, arbitration, or litigation to help get beyond whatever may be hindering resolution.

MEDIATION

In mediation, you and your spouse would meet (either by yourselves or with your attorneys present) with a mediator who will help facilitate the discussion and resolution of your outstanding issues. How? They may present and help weigh options and may use conflict resolution (de-escalation) techniques to lower tensions and move you through conflict and into closure. Under no circumstances, however, does the mediator *ever* provide legal advice to either of you. For this reason, many people prefer to attend mediation *with* their attorneys, so they can immediately understand and analyze the legal implications of the various options presented.

Some mediators, if requested, will use what is known as *evaluative mediation*, which means that they may weigh in with an opinion as to how they think a court *might* rule on a particular issue. This can be very helpful in ultimately resolving a contested issue, especially if the mediator is a retired judge or an experienced trial attorney.

It's also good to be aware that some attorneys do not like evaluative mediation. These folks believe that a mediator's opinion steps on your decision-making toes, and may either unfairly affect the outcome of the mediation or frustrate the process by diluting the mediator's appearance of neutrality.

Personally, I like evaluative mediation. Why? I have found that a candid evaluation from the mediator, especially if the mediator is a retired judicial officer in the jurisdiction in which the case would be tried, often settles the case. And presumably, you're attending mediation to try and settle your case. Sometimes a simple reality check is all that is needed to take the air out of puffed-up positions that are, at their core, unreasonable or legally unwarranted. This reality check can save you significant time, uncertainty, attorneys' fees, and other additional costs that are involved in litigating a contested issue to final resolution.

Also, it is important to note that mediation is a voluntary process; because of this, settlement will not be forced upon either one of you. In fact, mediation can sometimes be frustrating for this very reason. Occasionally, you think you may have reached settlement during the mediation, only to find afterward that your spouse has decided to back away from the agreement. In an effort to prevent this, many mediators will write up a summary of the agreements reached at mediation, which will be signed by you, your spouse, your attorneys (if you two are represented), and the mediator. The purpose behind this is that, in many jurisdictions, these written summaries can be enforceable in court if one of you attempts to renege on the deal.

Take note of this, and remember to ask a prospective mediator whether he or she will write a mediation summary at the end of the session—which will be signed by everyone—if any agreements are reached. I believe this is important, not only for the reason mentioned earlier, but also because mediators are *not* free. They regularly charge as much as, or more than, the attorneys representing you. Though their fees are usually shared between you and your spouse, or paid with a marital asset (a check from the joint checking account, for example), mediation is an investment—in the mediator's time and in your time, as well. I like to see a written summary at the end of mediation outlining *any* resolved issues, even if we were only able to reach a partial settlement.

ARBITRATION

Arbitration feels a lot like court, but instead of a judge who makes the decisions, an arbitrator is handpicked by the divorcing couple to resolve any contested issues. So, if you want the china, and your spouse wants the china, then the arbitrator decides who gets it.

Sometimes a couple will hire an arbitrator to do what's called *mediation-arbitration* (also known as *med-arb*). In this hybrid process, the arbitrator helps the couple get as close to settlement as possible using mediation principles. If the couple reaches an impasse on a certain issue, then the arbitrator can "break the tie," and decide the contested issue. This decision can be binding or nonbinding, depending upon what the couple agrees to at the outset of the process.

Most often in my practice, I use arbitration to assist clients in resolving contested minor issues, like the division of household goods and furnishings. I prefer for both sides, if at all possible, to reach their own decisions concerning "the big issues" (like custody, parenting time, child support, and spousal maintenance). It seems to work better, in the long run, if my clients and their spouses have actively contributed to reaching a settlement. When you have both a stake and a say in the process, you will feel more empowered and satisfied with the final outcome.

Clients who rely on an arbitrator, or the court, to dictate resolutions are often unhappy with the outcome. Why? The decision-maker must work within a certain set of laws, which often leaves little room for flexibility and creative solutions. And what's more, decision-makers tend to balance interests between you and your spouse, so neither of you "wins" or "loses" on every issue. The result of this is that it becomes very easy to blame the decision-maker for an unsatisfactory result, which tends to fuel—not quell—the overall anger and frustration that can accompany a divorce.

LITIGATION

Litigation is a process in which you and your spouse look to the court for help to resolve the divorce. Sometimes you may need the court to make a decision on your behalf with regard to a contested issue. Other times, you might just need the structure of the court process to keep everyone moving forward toward the goal of becoming divorced. Occasionally, though, you may need direction from the court, in the form of the judge's opinion on a certain issue, or a referral to some sort of outside process or service, such as an early neutral evaluation (if available) or a custody evaluation. The judge's opinion, and/or the input from the process or service, may assist in resolving the contested issue—which might, in turn, resolve the whole case—so that no further intervention from the court is necessary.

The extent of available court-referral services varies from jurisdiction to jurisdiction. Some districts have a host of services to help the divorcing couple or have enough money to provide some of the court-related services, many of which are fee based, and some of which may be free. Others refer divorcing couples to private service providers because their district has no funding to provide these services. In any event, it is important to research and learn what services may be available in your own jurisdiction.

Regardless, very few cases end up at trial before a judge. Fewer than 5 percent of all divorce cases end up in trial. This number is so small because the costs (financial and emotional) of going to trial are very high.

Why is it so expensive? Well, there is a lot of time involved in going to trial, and attorneys bill for their time. And the route to trial is rarely streamlined and straightforward. Usually, there are several court appearances before trial. In my own home jurisdiction, we have a first appearance (called an *initial case management conference*), followed occasionally by a temporary hearing, followed by one or more status phone conferences with the judicial officer assigned to the case, followed by a pretrial conference (where the judge meets with the divorcing couple and their respective attorneys to help resolve the case, if possible), followed finally, by trial, if necessary. As you can see, there are many steps to this process, and the distance between the steps is usually measured in *months*. Summed up, the process is lengthy and will be both an emotional and financial drain.

In a final trial, usually a judge, and not a jury, hears the case and ultimately renders a decision. Everyone has to be present at trial—you, your soon-to-be ex-spouse, both of your attorneys, and any witnesses you intend to call. The judge accepts evidence, in the forms of testimony and documentation. When all of the evidence has been presented, the judge often takes the matter "under advisement," and issues a written decision (often called a *judgment and decree*) at a later date. In fact, it is commonplace for a written decision to be issued *several months* after the trial is concluded. In most cases, you will likely walk away from trial without any formal conclusion about the details of your divorce.

Rarely is there an in-court, dramatic revelation of the outcome by the judge—contrary to what television or movies sometimes show! The reason judges tend to take the evidence "under advisement" is because they need to review and reflect on the information presented at trial before coming to a final decision. In short, the court is not generally "ready" to issue a final decision as to the outcome of the case in the courtroom at the end of trial.

In a trial situation, the court may ask for both of you to submit a proposed judgment and decree, either prior to, or more likely, *after* your trial. Seeing both of your proposed end-goals for the divorce may help the court more quickly enter the final judgment and decree.

Before each court appearance, you'll almost always need to prepare and file legal paperwork called *pleadings*. Pleadings formally convey information to the court, and request the court to take action. These documents take time to prepare and file, especially when getting ready for trial. So, in addition to charging for the preparation time, attorneys also charge you—often on an hourly basis—for their *attendance* at court appearances. Also, there will likely be many meetings between an attorney and client during contested litigation, as well as many meetings between the attorneys themselves, and meetings between the attorneys and other professionals who are helping prepare the case (think paralegals, accountants, and therapists), as well as court fees. So, just as the saying goes: time is money . . . and all of this time adds up. Contested litigation can easily cost tens of thousands of dollars. For this reason, many divorcing people seek to avoid it.

Extended litigation—often referred to as protracted or high-conflict litigation— is also emotionally expensive. I see many clients underestimate the emotional wear and tear that extended litigation takes on them, their spouses, and their children. In fact, the research shows that kids fair the worst in divorces that are hostile and drawn-out. In these cases, I've regularly seen children decline—in both school and their social circles—as if they've launched their emotions right off the edge of a cliff. Children literally act out their pain and grief, so it is more common than not for them to have dramatic and negative shifts in behavior during the throes of a bitter and protracted divorce.

If this prognosis for children seems halting or shocking, consider this: statistics show that protracted, litigated divorces can make either party (or both parties) more anxious, depressed, and angry—even long after the divorce itself is concluded. Sounds fun, doesn't it?

Then why do people engage in protracted litigation? Again, it is good to remember that few actually do. As I mentioned earlier, only a small percentage (approximately 5 percent) of divorcing couples actually end up going to trial. When a divorce heads down this path, it's often because at least one party is being unreasonable. I say this because an honest-to-goodness, good faith, difference of opinion on a certain issue can be straightforwardly resolved *well* short of trial, through evaluative mediation, mediation-arbitration, or arbitration. And it is also possible that this drawn-out struggle arises because either one—or both—of you isn't ready to be divorced quite yet. This engagement—which is the last bastion of intimacy for a divorcing couple—prolongs the final dissolution of the bonds of matrimony.

Who Chooses the Process and How Does the Process Begin?

There is no one right process for every divorcing couple. Ideally, you and your spouse would discuss the various options (after one or both of you have met with an attorney and learned about the options), and select the one that best meets your family's particular needs. More often, though, I've seen the initiating party choose a process (say litigation), without input or direction from their spouse.

That's not to say that all processes are mutually exclusive, although some are. For example, a divorcing couple can't both litigate *and* be in the middle of a Collaborative Law case. Both parties could, though, use mediation during either the process of Collaborative Law or litigation, if an impasse were to arise.

Regardless, almost all divorces start the same way—with the preparation of a summons and petition (or a joint petition if the couple is amicable and jointly wants to apply for the divorce). When a summons and petition are used, formal delivery (called *service of process*) of these documents upon the other spouse is required. The delivery of these documents *must* be done by someone *other* than the initiating spouse, unless the receiving spouse agrees to accept service in a different manner, like through email or regular mail. The reason for this is simple: the judicial system wants to make sure that each of you has been notified of the divorce proceeding and has an opportunity to respond.

Additionally, the judicial system does not want to put the responsibility of notifying the receiving spouse in the *literal* hands of the initiating spouse. The system is designed this way to prevent the initiating spouse from lying about having notified the soon-to-be ex-spouse. Why would an initiating spouse ever lie about this? Well, if the receiving spouse doesn't respond to the proceeding, then the initiating spouse can proceed to complete the divorce based on the receiving spouse's *default* (failure to respond). When this occurs, the initiating spouse often gets an outcome that mirrors what he or she has requested in the petition, which is often drafted to favor the initiating spouse. So, the judicial system wants to remove the opportunity for the initiating spouse to lie about having given notice of the proceeding to the other party, in an attempt to orchestrate a favorable outcome. This would be akin to rigging the deck in a card game and winning by trickery, and the judicial system absolutely abhors fraud, especially when someone is deliberately "left out of the game" by the opposing spouse.

What Are the Summons and Petition?

The *summons* is a short document (usually two or three pages) that alerts the other spouse to the fact that the divorce process is beginning. It usually contains what are called *restraining provisions*. These provisions set forth actions that *cannot* occur once the summons has been served to the other spouse. These include, for example, cancelling insurance policies or changing insurance beneficiary designations. The summons also generally forbids the liquidation of assets without the consent of the other spouse, unless the liquidation is necessary either to provide for the necessities of life or to retain an attorney.

While the summons gives notice that the divorce process has begun, as well as certain "no-no's" during the divorce, the *petition* is a different entity altogether. The petition is designed to give the court an initial thumbnail sketch of the lay of the marital landscape, and it is used as a reference document for the courts. It often ranges from five to seven pages, and lays out the basic information about the divorcing couple and their family, such as full legal names and dates of birth of the spouses and their children, both spouses' addresses, as well as a relatively short, and usually unspecific, inclusion of your assets and liabilities. The petition will also often list each spouse's respective employer and job title, in addition to the earnings derived from each spouse's employment.

Bear with me—lastly, at the end of the petition, there is a clause known as the *prayer for relief* or the *wherefore clause*, in which the petitioner (whomever initiated the divorce) spells out, in *simple terms*, how he or she would prefer the issues within the divorce to be resolved. The wherefore clause is usually drafted as the initiating spouse's "best case scenario." This is because the initiating spouse is usually limited to the relief they can get from the court by the requests contained in the wherefore clause. So if you're the responding spouse, don't be mortified if the prayer for relief or wherefore clause seems to be stilted in the direction of the initiating spouse. It almost always is, for the reasons detailed above.

Service of Process

Before we move forward, know that the summons and petition get served to the receiving spouse in one of two ways: 1) the delivery of the documents to the other spouse by someone *other than* the initiating spouse (for the reasons discussed earlier); or 2) the other spouse's willingness to admit to service by other means (such as email or mail) and by signing a document called an admission of service. Once the summons and petition are served, the case begins.

Some people mistakenly believe that the case begins when the legal paperwork is filed with the court, but this isn't how it works. In fact, if you and your spouse have chosen to mediate, collaborate, or arbitrate, it is not unusual for attorneys to wait to file the paperwork with the court to avoid a "dual track" process, which may end up costing unnecessary additional time and money (in attending mediation sessions and also going to various court appearances). If you and your spouse are in mediation, for example, attorneys often wait to file the legal paperwork until there is a final settlement or the process breaks down and court intervention becomes necessary.

Discovery: Getting Information Formally or Informally

Once the process has been started, the next step is to exchange information (think tax returns, paycheck stubs, retirement account, and credit card statements). The process of exchanging information is called *discovery*. Discovery is a very important part of the divorce. Both you and your spouse need to understand each of the pieces of the puzzle (think income, budgets, assets, liabilities) to make *informed* decisions about your future. Further, property settlements tend to be *final*, and generally cannot be reopened at a later date if you have second thoughts about an asset's value or allocation. Given this, you need to do your homework on the front-end during the divorce.

Discovery can be either informal or formal. Informal discovery is done by a simple request for information, and is exchanged—most commonly—by letter or by email. So, your spouse's attorney may write your attorney a letter, requesting information from you (like tax returns, paycheck stubs, health insurance information, and your monthly living expenses). Your attorney would then write back to your spouse's attorney, requesting similar information. If you're not represented by an attorney, then you would request this information directly from your spouse, and vice versa.

In formal discovery, court pleadings are used to elicit information, most commonly in the forms of written questions (called *interrogatories*) and requests for copies of certain information (called a *request for production of documents*). Once the formal discovery request is received, it has to be answered within a certain period of time—usually thirty days. Also, the formal answers to interrogatories have to be sworn to under oath by the responding spouse.

Given the time restrictions and the requirement to sign the answers under oath, formal discovery is often used for one of two reasons. First, if you are concerned that your spouse will not provide the information in a timely manner, you may choose to use formal discovery. Formal discovery is also used when there are concerns that the other spouse may misrepresent the truth (thus necessitating formal answers under oath). Many spouses, however, do not have these concerns and choose not to spend money having their attorneys draft formal legal pleadings to exchange information. Courts may also prefer to use informal discovery as a way to help keep costs down and to avoid inflaming anger between the divorcing couple. Formal discovery has the potential to add conflict and animosity between the spouses. Why? No one likes paying the additional costs associated with formal discovery, and few people like having their integrity called into question by being required to answer formal questions under oath.

Regardless of how the information is obtained, each of you needs to be made aware of *all* the assets, liabilities, incomes, and monthly expenses. Only then can you have an effective discussion as to who should get what, who should pay child support and how much, and so forth. In this stage, it is not uncommon for divorcing couples to want to speed ahead and negotiate a global resolution before all the facts are known. This inclination to rush forward and conclude the divorce through a negotiation that is ignorant of some (or many) of the facts can actually have disastrous results, and can lead to setbacks that protract—not shorten—the length of the divorce.

When a divorcing couple quickly settles without all of the facts, chances are they may find it difficult to secure an attorney who is willing to draft or submit court paperwork on their behalf. This is because most attorneys follow the practice of *due diligence*. Due diligence is a process in which the attorney comes to understand all the facts of the case—not just the clients' agreements on various issues. Think of due diligence as informal discovery done by the attorney. You may be wondering, "Why does the attorney need to do this if my spouse and I have settled our case? Seems like a waste of *our* time and money." I see your point, but few attorneys will engage in (or draft legal paperwork memorializing) "horse trading" without having conducted their own due diligence review. Why? One word: malpractice. Most attorneys will not take the risk that the client may later develop "buyer's remorse," and then sue the attorney for failing to insist upon due diligence. Long story short, most attorneys will insist on slowing down the process to allow for the full disclosure of all important facts.

Even if the divorcing spouses choose not to be represented, often the court will want to know all the pertinent facts before signing off on the final divorce paperwork. In fact, in the jurisdiction where I practice, couples who represent themselves and fill out their own divorce paperwork have to attach copies of all pertinent financial documentation (like tax returns, paycheck stubs, and 401(k) statements) for the court's review. Why? Overall, the court wants to ensure equity in the process of divorce, and that no one is taken advantage of (intentionally or unintentionally) through their own ignorance.

Despite this, I will occasionally encounter people who do not want to disclose all of their income or assets for fear that they will have to share them with their spouse. These folks usually hide or misrepresent the extent of their income or the assets. This is a bad idea for several reasons. First, failing to participate in full disclosure amounts to committing fraud upon the court and can have very serious ramifications. In addition, assets that are left out of the divorce paperwork are called *omitted assets*. If discovered, these assets can be taken from the nondisclosing spouse and awarded to the other. And the court also has the power to punish the nondisclosing individual by ordering the payment of the other spouse's attorney's fees, in addition to whatever court costs have been incurred. So, honesty really is the best—and least expensive—policy.

After discovery is exchanged, both of you will then often participate in one of the dispute-resolution processes outlined earlier (such as mediation or arbitration) to work through any differences you may have regarding either social issues (custody and parenting time) or financial issues (child and spousal support, property allocation). Sometimes, though, there may be such a large difference of opinion over an issue (say custody of the children), that the divorcing couple may need some initial feedback on their perspectives before diving into the dispute-resolution processes. Getting this feedback can be achieved in one of several ways, and it varies by jurisdiction.

Some jurisdictions offer initial opinions from seasoned social or financial evaluators after they've heard from both sides. (This process is often called an *early neutral evaluation*). If, however, your concerns cannot be resolved with initial feedback from a process like this, then a full-blown evaluation (like a custody study or business valuation) may be necessary.

For example, a custody evaluation is an in-depth study of the family. The evaluation is usually conducted by an experienced social worker, psychologist, or family law attorney, and sometimes by a *guardian ad litem* who is appointed to determine the best interests of the children. The evaluator will usually interview you and your spouse, your children, and often collateral contacts (such as therapists or day care providers). The evaluator may also want to consider additional information, like chemical dependency or psychological evaluations. Ultimately, the evaluator makes written recommendations regarding what custody and parenting time arrangements are in the best interests of the minor children.

Clients often experience custody evaluations as invasive, long, win/lose, polarizing, and *expensive*. Nonetheless, they can be helpful when clients are stuck in what appears to be an intractable impasse concerning custodial placement and parenting time schedules.

Sometimes a couple doesn't need a full-blown evaluation to be able to come to an agreement. You and your spouse may just have a difference of opinion, which could be resolved with a little feedback from the decision-maker in your case. Occasionally, some judicial officers will share their impressions regarding a contested issue. This is often done informally, such as in a conversation with both of your attorneys. If available, this option can be very helpful, as there is nothing quite like "hearing it from the horse's mouth," so to speak. If you get a pretty good idea as to what the judge might do at trial, then why proceed to trial? Good, bad, or indifferent, insight as to how the judge would likely rule on a particular issue will often help you settle on terms that reflect the judge's input.

Once a settlement is reached on all issues, or upon the conclusion of a final trial in the matter, the court will issue a *judgment and decree of dissolution*. This document varies from state to state, but often contains all of the facts that form the basis for the agreement (or decision, if the case is tried), which are usually referred to as *findings of fact*, as well as the agreement (or decision) itself, which are usually set forth as *conclusions of law*.

If you have a final trial in your case, as discussed earlier, both attorneys will usually draft proposed judgment and decrees, which reflect the way in which their respective clients would like the case resolved. The court then chooses from among these proposals, and then edits the document to reflect the court's decision with respect to all contested issues. If you go to trial, and neither you nor your spouse is represented, then the court will prepare your judgment and decree.

If your judgment and decree is the result of an agreement between you and your spouse, then one of your attorneys (or one of you, if neither of you is represented) will be responsible for preparing the document. The judgment and decree usually needs to be signed by both parties in the presence of a notary public, and also by your respective attorneys, if you and/or your spouse are represented.

Once it is fully executed, the document will be submitted to the court for its review and the judge's signature. Once the judge reviews and signs the judgment and decree, it is usually handed off to the court administrator, who enters the judgment on the judgment roll. At this point, your divorce is finalized. You (or your attorney on your behalf) will get notice of its finality. Some jurisdictions send out a written notice that basically says, "You're divorced." Other jurisdictions send out an uncertified copy of the final judgment and decree.

How Long?

So, how long does this whole process take, anyway? The honest answer is, "It depends." It depends on how amenable each person is to resolving the concerns related to the divorce, which often correlates to how ready each is to be divorced. It also depends on how complex the case is. If, for example, you have several businesses that need to be appraised, or premarital interests that have to be traced, then these issues may need time to get unwrapped and evaluated before a final resolution can take place.

That said, a divorce can also go very quickly. If both of you agree on all the issues, then the only factors driving the date of the final divorce are: 1) how quickly the paperwork can be drafted; 2) how quickly the court will process the paperwork; and 3) whether there is a waiting provision in your state prior to the entry of the judgment and decree. A divorce can be finalized in as little as two weeks. This is the exception, however, and not the rule. It is more common for divorces to take an average of six to nine months. Divorce can take even longer than this, unfortunately, if there are many complex or contested issues that simply defy straightforward resolution. In these cases, it is not uncommon for the divorce to take a year to eighteen months to complete. And to reiterate, lengthy, drawn-out divorces take a toll on *everyone* involved . . . and they are expensive! Both the emotional and financial costs of divorce tend to increase exponentially the longer the divorce takes.

What Would Love Do?

Every client wants to know: "What's the key to getting through this process as best as possible?" After almost twenty years of practicing law, I now believe the answer is a pretty simple—yet profound—filter that can guide every decision, every action in divorce: What would love do?

This question is the mantra behind the organization of the same name. What Would Love Do International was founded by Christine Horner in response to a call from the United Nations for video submissions to the question, "What would you do to make this world a better and safer place?"

Ms. Horner's response was simple: to make choices from a place of love, as opposed to fear.

So, what if you were to apply this perspective when making decisions in your divorce? Personally, I believe that applying this perspective is the way to get through the divorce with the least amount of pain. The issue, of course, is how on earth, in the midst of all the emotions that are part and parcel of divorce (especially a contentious one), do you do this?

Choosing love *does not* mean being a martyr, falling on your sword as the saying goes, and giving up everything. No. Choosing love starts with you loving you. Self-love is not selfish. It is as vital as the air we breathe or the water we drink. Self-love in divorce means first evaluating what options are best for you, *before* you consider what options are best for your kids or your spouse. For many divorcing people, especially women, this practice is often new, scary, and uncomfortable. Many women, and some men, have put others' needs—their kids, their spouse, and even their dog—first for years.

Instead of putting everyone else's needs first, you must start with putting your needs first, and evaluating the options and possible action steps from this perspective. This does not mean that you will make decisions solely from this place, because decisions in divorce are often textured and layered and require a weighing and balancing of needs and interests. What I am saying is this: what is important to you must be identified first, and included as an *integral* part of this weighing and balancing of needs and interests.

Once you have started with honoring your needs and interests from a place of love, I recommend evaluating *every* issue, decision, or circumstance from the perspective of love.

Let's say, for example, that your soon-to-be ex-spouse is almost an hour late in getting the kids to you at the end of parenting time. You decide that self-love dictates an honest response: you are mad at this development. What would love do with respect to the kids' needs in this situation? Kids don't want to watch their parents fight or bicker, so a calm transition, without addressing the issue in their presence, is probably warranted. Fair enough. But you still want to address your spouse's tardiness. Love might ask the question, "Why were you tardy?" Love might recognize that despite the best of intentions, "stuff" occasionally happens, plans change, and people are late. Love may also know that a hostile confrontation and shaming won't shore up any future tardiness, that's for certain.

Love might simply ask for what it needs.

So in this circumstance, after consideration of these perspectives, maybe you send an email to your spouse that says, "I was torqued you were an hour late tonight with the kids. I didn't want to make them feel uncomfortable, so I didn't address this with you at the exchange. Why were you late? I know that it is sometimes impossible to get anywhere on time with our three kids, especially if one of them is sick. While I do expect you to be on time for our exchanges, if you run late, please text me and let me know this. I'd also appreciate knowing why you are running late, so I don't make up a bunch of stories. Thanks."

I am in no way, shape, or form saying that any of this is easy. Far from it. In divorce, we say that the best predictor of future behavior is past behavior. That is to say, people tend to act from what's *familiar*, and continue to make decisions from a triggered place of negative, self-limiting beliefs and habituated patterns. In other words, it's easy to reflexively choose from the same place—and the same perspective—that got you to the threshold of divorce in the first place.

So now, the question becomes: How do I step out of those reactive, reflexive, old-school beliefs and patterns?

The answer is: you need to buy yourself time—somehow, some way. Even a moment or two can make a huge difference, but preferably an hour, or a day. In my experience, *immediate* responses tend to be *reactive*. Even if you have to bite your tongue, just wait to reply. Buy yourself some time to let the emotions wash through you, so you can step out of a knee-jerk reaction, and choose to respond from a place of love.

Operating from the perspective of what would love do is not easy in divorce. But it's not impossible. Every day, I see clients who choose to navigate divorce from a place of loving themselves, their kids, and their spouses, even when it's uncomfortable, even when a part of them would like to lash out, even when they feel hurt and betrayed. These same clients, perhaps not surprisingly, also tend to get through their divorces "better"—which is to say more quickly, more cost-effectively, and less painfully. So if you want a better experience of divorce, as ironic as that may sound, choose love.

Having the Hard Conversation

Who loves conflict? Raise your hands. Anyone? I didn't think so.

Most of my clients, and most people in general, tend to avoid conflict whenever and wherever possible.

In divorce, though, you're not going be able to avoid conflict. Even in an uncontested divorce, where all the issues are agreed upon, there was still likely a hard conversation that started the whole process! One or both of you had to acknowledge that the marriage was over.

Being vulnerable and sharing what may be an unpopular perspective is hard. But your life will not change unless you are willing to do something about it. You either live in service to your future, or you sabotage it. If you do nothing differently, your future will look exactly the same as your past. I think it was Brené Brown who once said that the quality of your life depends upon the number of hard conversations you're willing to have.

So just how do you tell someone you don't want to be married to them anymore? How do you say to your wife that you're worried about her drinking, and are concerned that the kids are not safe around her? How do you open up a dialogue with your spouse about your fifteen-year-old daughter, who has started cutting herself? How do you request spousal maintenance (alimony) from your husband, when all the major fights with him over the last ten years have revolved around how you spent money?

First, take a breath and acknowledge that this isn't easy stuff. Give yourself permission to be scared. Give yourself permission to have the hard conversation *anyway.*

Following is the process that I suggest. It is an amalgam of several articles from several different psychologists and relationship experts, mixed with my own experience as a divorce attorney.

1. Ask your spouse for time to talk. Let him or her know the reason for the conversation. Don't hide the ball. No one likes a heavy conversation sprung on them.

2. Choose the place for the conversation. Some of my clients have the hard conversation with their spouses at home after the kids have gone to bed. Some have them over the phone. Other clients to go out to dinner at a restaurant that is quiet enough for a personal conversation, but in a public place where outbursts or reactions will probably be socially constrained.

3. Set some ground rules. You may want to say, "I would like you to listen to me for five minutes, without interrupting, and I will listen to you for five minutes, without interrupting." You may also want to agree that there will be no swearing and no yelling. Make your expectations clear for how you want the communication to occur.

4. Limit the conversation to the hard issue. If you're going to tell your spouse that you no longer want to be married, don't also bring up that he forgot to take out the trash this morning. Don't cloud the one major issue. It is too easy to get off on a tangent and avoid talking about the real issue.

5. Have a soft startup. What does this mean? It means saying, "This is hard for me to say, but I need to share something with you," versus, "You're a jerk, and I'm leaving you!" Gentleness goes a long way in a hard conversation.

6. Focus on your feelings. Make "I" statements. Describe what's happening for you. "I feel frustrated, because it seems like my needs are consistently unmet." Keep it about yourself, your needs, and your interests. Avoid blaming your spouse. "You never touch me anymore" is better stated as, "I need touch and affection, and I'm not getting these needs met." Blaming your spouse will only raise his or her hackles, and the conversation will likely devolve into an argument. Your spouse will be too busy in defense mode, and won't be able to hear what you have to say.

7. Politeness and appreciation go a long way. So does "I'm sorry." A hard conversation can soften with a little acknowledgment. "My dissatisfaction with our relationship has nothing to do with our children. You're a great dad to the kids."

8. Let your spouse have their response. Few people enjoy disappointing or hurting someone else. It is hard, even when a relationship is over, to sit with your spouse's emotions. As long as the response doesn't threaten or hurt you, your spouse gets to respond. Even if you disagree with the response, I suggest hearing it and acknowledging it. This sets a precedent of respect for future hard conversations, which you will be having, especially if you have children together.

9. Suggest and, if possible, agree upon the next steps. Maybe your conversation leads you and your spouse to decide to try marriage counseling. Perhaps your spouse acknowledges that the marriage is over and offers to contact a divorce attorney to get the ball rolling. Simply put, there's some comfort in knowing what comes next.

Truth is, I know that having a hard conversation with your spouse is difficult, even under the best of circumstances. When the stakes are even higher, though, like when you need to broach the topic of divorce, it's good to have a plan for how to best navigate the conversation. Use these nine steps to plan for, and successfully have, the hard conversations with your spouse.

Now that you have the basic lay of the land with what may be in front of you as you head down the path of divorce, it's important to step back, and take both a breath and a moment to consider how you're feeling. You've just read through the whole process—in all of its iterations—in this one chapter, so I get that you might be overwhelmed. That's okay.

Whether or not that's the case, once you feel ready, ask yourself the following questions.

1. Have I clearly and kindly communicated to my spouse that I would like to begin the separation and/or divorce proceedings? If not, am I ready to make a tangible move

in that direction? What can I do to safely plan for having that hard conversation?

2. Once the hard conversation has been had, what kind of divorce process feels best for our situation?

3. What are *my* needs? How can I best go into this next season in my life from a place of love—loving myself, my children, and then others? (Be *clear* on what you need to take care of yourself during this time and moving forward so that you can respond from a place of love. Remember that you are of no good to your children if you yourself are depleted, spread thin, angry, overtired, or high strung. If you can love yourself first, that love can extend to those around you. And even though the process of divorce contains grieving, choosing love will allow you to navigate it more wholly and quickly.)

Hiring a (Good) Family Law Attorney

Do I Need an Attorney?

Many people divorce without ever having to spend a dollar in attorney's fees. In fact, I have met with many prospective clients only to tell them, "You really don't need my services if you're willing to do the work yourself." I help point the prospective clients in the right direction, and they end up preparing and filing their own divorce paperwork at a fraction of the cost they would have spent on my services.

Bad for business? Absolutely not. Prospective clients who are not "upsold" on legal services tend to be very happy with the information and direction I provide, and often refer other clients who do indeed need my services. But, as you might imagine, the DIY divorce is not an option in every case.

So how do you know when you need an attorney and when you don't? The cases that most commonly *do not* need an attorney have two defining characteristics.

First, these cases tend to be about the division of assets and liabilities. Usually, the couple has no children, and spousal maintenance isn't an issue because each individual is self-supporting. In addition, the assets and debts—such as 401(k)s, the house, and the cars—are pretty easy to identify and value, and both parties are knowledgeable about all of the assets and liabilities of the marriage.

The second characteristic is that the divorcing couple is relatively amicable, and they have figured out how to divide their marital estate. Some of these folks have been separated awhile and have worked through the emotions of divorce. Others have been living together as "roommates," and there is a mutual understanding that the marriage is over—and has been for some time. Neither person blames the other for the divorce. Instead, both people have a common goal—to finish the divorce proceeding as cost-effectively as possible.

When people with cases like these show up in my office, I give them information about the resources available for the DIY option. In Minnesota, for example, individuals can get the divorce paperwork online, fill it all out, and then file it in the county in which they reside. This process is straightforward and relatively easy when the spouses are amicable and have figured out how to divide their resources.

Even if you plan to do it yourself, it may be a good idea to have a short consultation with an attorney. The purpose of the meeting is twofold: 1) to have the attorney quickly review the paperwork to ensure that it has been filled out correctly (so that it can be processed properly by the court), and 2) to have the attorney share any overarching thoughts or concerns he or she may have about the agreement. This does not mean, however, that the attorney will be signing off on your paperwork. The attorney is simply giving you an opinion as to how the agreement matches up with the law in your state.

What if I Cannot Afford an Attorney?

What if your case does not fall into the DIY category, and you cannot afford to hire an attorney to represent you? Take heart! You do have options!

First, you may qualify for free or reduced-cost legal services. These are often referred to as *legal assistance programs*, and information about them can usually be found through your state's bar association. It is not uncommon for there to be several legal assistance programs—so check each of them out to see if one may apply to your circumstance.

While access to free legal services varies considerably by jurisdiction, usually there is an income qualification threshold. If you qualify for services, there is probably a waiting list, too. There may also be volunteer programs that are run at the county or city level (or even privately), so do some research to find out what public and private services may be available to you.

Also, attorneys will occasionally discount their rates (often referred to as a *sliding fee scale*) to provide access to representation for clients who could not otherwise afford a lawyer. If this may apply to your circumstance, be sure to inquire about this when you interview prospective attorneys.

If you do not qualify for free or reduced-cost ongoing legal representation, then you may want to look into what are known as *unbundled legal services* (also known as *limited scope representation* or *discrete task representation*). This is a method of legal representation in which the attorney and client agree to limit the attorney's involvement in the divorce to help save the client money. For example, you may want an attorney to draft certain legal paperwork for you. Or perhaps you have an upcoming court appearance and want legal coaching to prepare for your hearing. You could hire the attorney for these limited tasks, which are often billed through a flat fee (as opposed to an hourly rate).

If you do not qualify for free or reduced-cost legal services, and cannot afford to purchase any legal services (including unbundled legal services), then you are going to be your own attorney in your divorce. If this is what it comes to, then be your own best advocate. Get on the Internet. Do your research. There is a lot of information available out there. Find out what the divorce laws in your state say about custody, spousal maintenance (alimony), and property division. Search out a free or low cost divorce information seminar. Locate an attorney who will meet with you and give you a free initial consultation so you can learn more about the divorce laws in your state and how they may apply to your circumstance.

Not all divorcing couples agree on how to resolve the issues that are particular to their divorce. And, not all divorces are simple. Some divorces can have complex financial or custody issues. And some people just want to delegate the drafting of their divorce paperwork because they have neither the time nor the energy to do it themselves.

Others entrust the drafting of the legal paperwork to attorneys to help ensure that the legal paperwork is drafted correctly and accurately captures the parties' intentions. In other instances, one spouse may hire an attorney because there is discomfort with the thought of negotiating with the other spouse or preparing the legal paperwork alone.

Regardless, once a decision is made to hire an attorney, then the questions become:

1. How do I find an attorney?

2. How do I know if she or he is a good attorney and right for me? Do I interview attorneys, and if so, what do I ask them?

3. How do I pay for an attorney's services?

Let's take these questions one at a time.

How Do I Find a Good Attorney?

First, how do you find an attorney? Most people tend to ask their friends, family, coworkers, clergy, or psychologist for a referral. And since divorce is now quite common, it is generally pretty easy to find a referral for one or more divorce attorneys. The benefit of getting a referral is that there is usually some sort of personal connection or personal experience that the person referring the attorney has had with the attorney. It may be that the person is a former client, and if so, this person can provide an assessment of the attorney's actual service. In other cases, the referring person may know the attorney professionally or by reputation.

Regardless, most people looking for a divorce attorney find it to be a very personal and important choice, and seek some sort of recommendation. In this way, it's not unlike going out to dinner in a city you are visiting. If you are trying to decide upon a restaurant, what are you likely to do? Ask for a recommendation. Maybe a friend has been to the city and can make a personal recommendation. Or maybe, you use an online resource to educate yourself about the options and read user reviews of the various establishments to determine which restaurant you want to try. In much the same way, most people try to get some sort of input about the various options, be they for restaurants or attorneys!

When this is not possible, which can happen (perhaps you're new to the particular jurisdiction in which you are going to get divorced), then you may be able to find an attorney through the local bar association. Often, the attorneys involved in the family law sections of their local bar associations tend to be active and knowledgeable in the practice of family law. You may also check to see if there's a local Collaborative Law organization, if this process appeals to you. Last, but certainly not least, many people find an attorney online. You may be able to learn a lot about the attorney through this method, and he or she may offer references or a free consultation so that you can measure their online personas against the real person.

How Do I Know if the Attorney Is a Good One and Right for Me?

Hiring a divorce attorney is like hiring your general practitioner—the doctor you are going to rely on for your ongoing medical care. One of the first things you would probably want to know about your prospective physician is whether he or she could relate to you and your needs, and whether the physician was friendly and pleasant. After all, you might have to work with the doctor on some very difficult issues, and I would hope you would choose someone who could be patient and kind with you. You would also want someone who could be honest with you, even when it's hard, such as if you were to face a scary diagnosis. I suspect you would want to feel that you could trust the physician, quite literally, with your life. You would also want the physician to be experienced, especially with respect to any health issues that you may have or may be confronting. And finally, I am sure you would feel more confident about choosing a particular doctor if he or she came highly regarded from more than one source, like a personal referral or an excellent rating from a reputable online resource.

Similarly, these qualities apply to selecting a "good" attorney who is "right" for you. The way you find out whether the attorney has these qualities is to interview him or her. Many divorce attorneys give free initial consultations to allow you to do just that—to interview them, as well as get general information about the process of divorce.

How many attorneys should you interview? As many as you need to find one who you know, intuitively, has the six characteristics described in the example about the physician: patient, kind, honest, trustworthy, experienced, and comes highly recommended (preferably by more than one person).

When you interview attorneys, I suggest having a list of written questions. You need to get a feel for the individuals, as well as their practice style and experience level. For example, you'll probably want to know how long they have been in practice. Is family law their only practice area? Are they experienced with the processes that appeal to you (such as Collaborative Law or mediation), and the issues present in your case (for example spousal maintenance or domestic abuse)? How many clients are they currently representing? Do they have time to take on your case? Do they have staff to help with the preparation of your case at a lower hourly rate? Can you expect to interact solely with your attorney, or will you have regular contact with a paralegal or associate attorney? You will also want to ask them all about the financial expectations regarding the billing and payment of attorney's fees (which we'll address in just a moment).

In assessing the attorney, you need to feel confident that this is someone with whom you can work for the next several months (or maybe a year or more), with contact as frequent as once a week or more. The attorney needs to be someone you trust has your best needs at heart, an experienced guide who can skillfully navigate your case through the shifting sands of the divorce process. If you do not have this confidence in your attorney, you will make what is an already emotionally difficult process even more treacherous by adding insecurity and second-guessing to the mix.

Before we move on to discuss how to pay for your attorney's services, I want to take a moment to address the experience level of a family law attorney. It is my personal opinion that novelty is a wonderful quality in certain things, such as trying out new restaurants and foods, sporting a new style or look, or being open to new experiences. I believe, however, that novelty is a decidedly bad idea when it comes to hiring an attorney who does not have the necessary experience with the issues that are a part of your divorce. This is particularly true if your case involves more complex issues, such as child abuse, spousal abuse, spousal maintenance, nonmarital claims, or a very extensive, high net-worth marital estate and income. Simply put, these just are not cases for beginners. There is too much at stake, and often the nuances gained over time—from practice—make all the difference in favorably resolving these cases.

By stating this, I am in no way disparaging newer family law attorneys. They generally do an excellent job for their clients. Newer attorneys are often the most familiar with recent developments in the law, and are commonly active in professional organizations and bar association activities to establish networking relationships. That said, if you select an attorney newer to the practice of family law, *and your case involves complex issues*, you might feel more secure with your representation if your attorney has an experienced colleague who can provide perspective, advice, or mentoring on these complex issues.

How Do I Pay for an Attorney's Services?

You have found an excellent attorney who is perfect for you. Great! Now, how do you pay for attorney's fees?

Suffice it to say, there aren't many people who open a "divorce savings account" at the outset of a marriage. Even once the marriage appears to be troubled, people don't generally start saving up for an attorney. Consequently, many people facing divorce often scramble to either come up with the retainer for the attorney, or to pay their attorney's fees on an ongoing basis. For a lot of my clients, the fear of how to pay for an attorney compounds the already difficult process of navigating divorce. If you're like most people, you're not sure how you're going to make it financially. You now have to support two separate homes (on the same combined income that used to support one household) *and* come up with extra money for the lawyers!

Yet even though this is the norm, most people don't qualify for free or reduced-fee legal services. So, if you want to be represented in your divorce, you're going to need to find a way to pay for the attorney's services.

When I meet with prospective clients, I share with them that there are actually several ways to pay for their attorneys. Most people seem to be surprised by this, but I think that's because the fear around the issue of fees clouds creative thought about how to pay for them. Most of my clients cannot pay for attorney's fees from their earnings alone (if you can, that's great), and that's where their analysis stops. During a divorce, however, the law generally allows parties to invade assets for the purpose of retaining an attorney, even though the use of the assets is otherwise restricted to meeting basic living expenses. For example, you might take a loan against your 401(k) to pay fees. Or, perhaps you decide to utilize a portion of the cash value of a whole life insurance policy to pay for fees. You may also choose to pay for your fees from a savings, checking, or investment account.

An important consideration in looking to an asset to help pay fees is whether you will incur taxes (either ordinary income or capital gains) by using the asset to pay for fees. Generally, it is not a good idea (unless you're retirement age) to liquidate a retirement plan, like a 401(k) or an IRA (individual retirement account), since you would incur a 10 percent prepayment penalty, in addition to state and federal income taxes. A better plan, often, is to use the funds in a qualified plan as security for a loan. In fact, many institutional retirement plans offer their employees loans against the retirement plan so that the employees don't have to remove the money from their retirement accounts and incur taxes and penalties. The great part of this option is that if you take a loan against your 401(k), the repayment of the loan replenishes your *own* retirement account. You're literally paying yourself back, as opposed to someone else.

People also take money from a line of credit (which is often secured by something, like the equity in their homes) and use it to pay attorney's fees. In fact, I have had many clients who, along with their spouses, jointly took out a line of credit to pay for each of their attorney's fees.

If you can't pay for your attorney's fees from your income or by accessing your assets (or if you have no assets), then there is another option to consider: financing the litigation and borrowing the funds. When my clients choose this option, they generally borrow funds from one of two sources, either from someone close to them (think parent, sibling, or best friend) or from their credit cards. But a word of caution here: both "lenders" are fraught with certain complications, so I would recommend these two options only as a last resort.

Borrowing money from family members and friends can come with a host of discomforts, from the timing of the repayment, to whether interest will be charged on the principle, to expectations about how the money will be used. Borrowing money from credit cards is not a cure-all either, as interest rates can be sky-high, and ongoing payments on the debt may not be affordable, especially once you are separated and living on your own (with or without help from your spouse). My advice to clients regarding financing their divorces is this: don't do it unless you can see a manageable way to repay the debt in a relatively short amount of time (a year or less) after your divorce, from either income or assets that will likely be awarded to you as a part of the divorce.

Many clients also ask about whether financing is available through me. That is, will I wait to get paid from the income or assets awarded to my client in the divorce. My answer is "no" for two reasons.

First, contingency fee arrangements in family law cases (where my fee is a certain percentage of whatever I obtain for you in assets and/or income from your divorce) are not allowed in the state in which I practice. Why? Because the Board of Professional Responsibility in my state does not want me to take a monetary interest that favors the dissolution of your marriage. In other words, the board doesn't want to promote divorces by giving attorneys a financial incentive to make sure their clients get divorced.

In addition, attorneys who are willing to be their clients' bankers are unwittingly entering into a conflict of interest (from my perspective), especially as the bill increases in size. When the attorney becomes a lender, she has to carry the debt, figure out whether to charge interest, and if so, how much. She also has to evaluate (just as institutional lenders do) the amount of credit the client can reasonably repay. In my opinion, this puts attorneys in a loyalty bind with their clients. Does the attorney-lender choose a legal strategy that reflects the client's best interest or the greatest likelihood of the attorney getting paid? Does the attorney withhold certain services, or discourage certain strategies, to a client who has a large balance?

Bottom line: don't choose your attorney to be your lender. Besides, many attorneys, like me, will refuse to play both roles.

HOW MUCH DOES IT REALLY COST?

So, how much does all this cost? Well, first of all, let's talk about how attorneys bill their clients.

Most divorce attorneys bill on an hourly basis, which is then multiplied by the amount of work done on the case. Many divorce attorneys also provide a detailed, itemized breakdown of the individual charges on your case, usually on a monthly basis. This way, you can see exactly what you're being billed for.

With regard to billing, the majority of family law attorneys send their clients a monthly statement. This statement contains either a summary of work performed on your case, or a detailed itemization. Most attorneys expect the monthly bill to be paid in full, and many require a retainer, which is money the client initially deposits with an attorney to pay for ongoing legal fees.

Retainers vary widely. They can be as little as $500 (which is unusual), and as much as $10,000. Attorneys are usually required to deposit retainer monies into a trust account for safekeeping. Most often, the retainer is debited once per month to pay for the attorney's fees and costs incurred in the previous month.

Retainers can be refundable if they are not used entirely; other retainers may not be entirely refundable. Retainers may also need to be replenished. This means if your retainer runs out, you need to fill up the retainer again. Some attorneys use what are called *evergreen retainers*. With this type of retainer, you make an initial deposit (say $5,000), which remains in the attorney's trust account. The attorney, however, does not use the retainer to pay your ongoing bill. Rather, you pay your bill on a monthly basis. If you fail to do so, then the evergreen retainer is used to pay your bill, and your representation is then usually terminated (for failing to keep your bill current). As you can see, it's very important to read the contract between you and your attorney and make sure that you clearly understand the fee arrangement, billing practices, and retainer requirements.

While most divorce attorneys bill on an hourly rate, some attorneys use flat-fee arrangements which I mentioned briefly earlier. This means the attorney will charge you a fixed fee for a fixed amount of work. For example, maybe you and your spouse have come to an agreement on all issues by yourselves. You feel, however, that you want to hire an attorney to draft the paperwork, to make sure that your agreement is accurately captured in writing. You decide to hire the attorney (who can usually only represent one spouse, not both spouses). He may quote you a flat, fixed fee for the preparation and filing of the paperwork. The representation is limited, since the attorney is not representing you on the entire case—just a portion of it—and so is the fee.

Flat fees tend to work best in cases in which there is no controversy. If all the attorney has to do is draft paperwork, or make a court appearance with you, then the attorney will be able to accurately measure this expense and may be willing to charge you a flat fee. Remember, though, that a flat fee is the same price whether the attorney spends many more hours on the case above and beyond his estimate or finishes the work in a lesser amount of time and has a higher profit margin.

If you are going to need representation throughout the course of the divorce, the attorney will most likely charge you an hourly rate. The amount of the hourly rate varies depending on factors such as the attorney's length of time in practice, the attorney's level of experience, the location of the divorce (there are higher rates for legal services in New York City than in Tuscaloosa, Alabama, for example), and so forth. Rates may vary from as little as $150 per hour for a relatively newer attorney to as high as $500 (or more) per hour for a very seasoned and highly sought-after divorce attorney.

So, how much time is your attorney going to spend at $200, $300, or $400 per hour? That is to say, how much is it going to cost overall? Unfortunately, there is no way the attorney can tell you the exact cost of representation.

"And why not," you ask?

There are too many factors beyond an attorney's control that will affect the cost of the divorce. For example, is your spouse going to be cooperative during the process? If so, the divorce will likely move along pretty quickly and cost less. If not, the divorce can drag on and on and cost a lot to finally resolve. Your attorney also has no control over the schedule or availability of the judge or mediator, the size of the court's caseload, or the manner in which the opposing attorney decides to handle your spouse's representation. Also, your attorney really has little control over you. And you can cost yourself a lot of money. (More on that in just a bit.)

My general rule of thumb regarding fees is what I call the *three bucket approach*. I tell prospective clients that about a third of my clients fall into the "first bucket," and spend less than $7,500 in attorney's fees on me—many spend significantly less. These clients often have no children, and have worked out the details of their divorce between themselves. I end up either reviewing the paperwork they have generated, or I become a scrivener and draft the divorce pleadings. There is relatively little animosity, as most of these folks have often been separated for a while, or have otherwise worked through the emotions related to divorce. The "second bucket" refers to those clients who spend between $7,500 and $15,000 in attorney's fees on me. These clients have contested issues which defy simple resolution. We may need to exchange discovery and attend mediation or participate in a few joint meetings (if it's a Collaborative Law case) before the parties are able to reach a global resolution to all issues. The "third bucket" refers to clients who spend in excess of $15,000 in attorney's fees on me. These clients may either have hotly contested issues or complicated ones, both of which tend to protract the case and drive up fees and costs.

Almost no one wants to have a large bill for attorney's fees. And almost all of my clients want to know what they can do to help minimize fees.

HOW DO I WORK WITH MY ATTORNEY AND MINIMIZE ATTORNEY'S FEES?

Every client not only wants to know how much the divorce is going to cost, but also how the financial costs can be minimized. I suggest three action steps they can take to help keep fees down.

Do the Stuff Your Attorney Asks You to Do

You will have certain "assignments" in your divorce. Initially, you will likely be asked to fill out a client questionnaire. You may also be asked to provide copies of certain documents, like paycheck stubs, income tax returns, and mortgage statements. Later on, you may be asked to provide answers or documentation in response to requests for information sought by the other side.

If you choose to undertake this work yourself, you can save yourself a lot of money. Do you want to track down a copy of the warranty deed to your house or would you like to pay my paralegal to do so? Would you like to do the initial draft of the answers to a formal set of questions received from the other side (interrogatories), or would you like me to do this on your behalf at my hourly rate? Simply put, delegating your own "assignments" to your attorney in the divorce will increase your attorney's fees and costs.

Sometimes, though, there is a good reason to delegate one or more "assignments." Some of my clients are busy professionals, and it is more cost-effective for them to delegate their divorce "assignments" and maintain their focus and productivity at work. Other clients are multitasking as it is (work, kids, church, extended family), and cannot add another item to their already extensive to-do lists.

Many of my clients do choose to delegate one or more "assignments" during their divorce. They do so knowing, however, that their fees and costs will be higher than if they had chosen to complete these items themselves.

Ask Your Attorney to Educate You

Many clients come to my office with no idea of what to expect as to the outcome of their divorce. Others have very fixed perspectives as to how their case "should" be resolved. Regardless, it is my responsibility to educate them about what they can expect from the divorce process and from the law, including the range of likely outcomes with respect to their kids, their money, and their property.

Generally speaking, no party walks away from the divorce "with it all." Divorce laws usually provide for some sort of sharing of the kids, the income, and the property acquired during the marriage.

This can come as quite a shock to some of my clients, especially to those who have a rigid perspective on how the divorce "should" be resolved. The "should" often reflects an implied desire by the client to be vindicated as a part of the divorce.

But the law rarely, if ever, helps one side "get even" with their spouse in the context of divorce. Regardless of how many vows your spouse may have broken, the law often sidesteps fault finding and, instead, focuses on how to move the family forward into separate households.

Moving the family forward is about sorting out parenting time schedules and budgets as well as the division of income and property. It does not usually involve admonishing one party for cheating on the other, and very seldom are there "paybacks" (in terms of getting more custody, parenting time, money, or property) for breaking the vows of marriage.

I suggest that you meet with your attorney relatively early on in your divorce to learn what the range of probable outcomes may be. Bring an open mind to the meeting. Ask questions of your attorney. Be prepared to hear information that may make you feel uncomfortable, disappointed, angry, or maybe even happy.

Once you are fully informed, if you decide to take an approach outside the range of likely outcomes outlined by your attorney, be prepared to open up your pocketbook. Why? A novel approach will usually be met with resistance by your spouse or their attorney. And when there is disagreement about the "best" or "most appropriate" resolution of one or more issues in the divorce, experts (like custody evaluators and appraisers) and court appearances are often needed, both of which are time consuming and expensive.

Tend to Your Emotional Needs Outside of the Legal Process

Divorce is jam-packed with emotions—even when the divorce is consensual and uncontested. It is a big transition, even if the marriage has been "dead" for years, and involves big emotions like grief, sadness, anger, disappointment, fear, anxiety, and excitement, among many, many others.

Regardless of whether you wanted the divorce or not, the process involves letting go of all the dreams you had for your marriage and coming to terms with beginning again. This is big stuff with which to grapple and emotionally unpack. Often, clients need time and space to sift through and process all these emotions.

But . . . you are not going to have either the time or the space to process these issues in your legal divorce. The legal process lays no claim to the emotions of divorce. Far from it. Truth be told, the legal divorce is really just a business transaction that involves negotiating the rights to the kids, the money, and the "stuff" (assets and liabilities) of your marriage.

Still, this does not stop some people from trying to get their emotional needs met through the legal process. Most commonly, I see this play out in one of two ways.

The first is when one spouse is enraged at the other spouse, usually for opting to leave the marriage or for breaking the vows of marriage. The enraged spouse attempts to throw up legal roadblock after legal roadblock in an attempt to make the divorce more painful (emotionally and financially) for the other spouse.

The second way this plays out is in a much more passive-aggressive fashion. In this scenario, one spouse does not want the marriage to end and chooses to be unresponsive in the process and uninterested in settling upon reasonable terms. Most often, this manifests as a desire by the client to retain more of the income or property ("Because I earned it" or "I deserve it because of what my spouse has done to me"). For example, it isn't unusual for a client to balk at the idea of paying spousal maintenance, especially if the client did not initiate the divorce. Regardless of the client's opinion about paying alimony, if there is a large disparity in the divorcing parties' incomes, spousal maintenance may be legally warranted. I have also had many a client who believed that he or she should be entitled to a larger share of the marital estate (property), because they were the spouse who worked outside of the home and "earned" it. This perspective, though, is not generally upheld by the law, which tends to see both spouses' contributions (whether working outside of the home or homemaking) as important to the acquisition of assets during the marriage.

These misperceptions can also play out with custody and parenting time issues. Sometimes, one parent has historically been the primary parent. This parent can sometimes believe that in divorce, she should have substantially more parenting time with the children. The law, once again, doesn't necessarily share this viewpoint. In most states, the law sees *both* parents' contributions to the children as important, and believes that *both* parents should have considerable parenting time with the children. Over the nearly twenty years I have been in practice, I have seen a huge shift toward joint parenting, with many parents equally sharing the duties of child rearing. I see this as the result of changes in our society. Both parents now commonly work outside of the home to help support the family. And so, there is no "stay-at-home" parent who does the majority of the parenting.

Regardless of how the circumstance plays out, clients who are being unreasonable are, underneath it all, scared. Scared of losing income, property, and, most importantly, time with the children. Divorce instigates change, and for some, these changes are unwelcome and just plain hard to get used to. I try to help my clients see that they can either cling to the fear or embrace the good parts of change and the adventure of this new life. Some cling to the old and others embrace the new. Clinging to the old, and trying to make the circumstance different from what it is, makes the process more uncomfortable for the client—and again, often more expensive. Be clear that both the aggressive and passive-aggressive attempts to get emotional needs met in the legal divorce drive up fees and costs. Both attempts try and defer the finality of the divorce, and really, the only way to drag it out is through disagreement.

When there is no agreement as to how much time each parent is to spend with the kids, or how the money and property is to be divided, then someone else (a judge or arbitrator) has to figure out these issues on the divorcing couple's behalf. This involves lots of legal paperwork, court appearances, waiting for court decisions, and sometimes even appeals. All of this takes time. And time is money.

I suggest the better use of resources is to take the emotional issues out of the legal process entirely. The best place to address and work through the difficult emotions of divorce is with the help of a reputable therapist or divorce coach.

You cannot control whether your spouse takes the emotional issues out of the legal process. You can, however, choose the avenue through which *you* deal with your emotions.

If you want to save money and keep your attorney's fees and costs down, you will work with a therapist or divorce coach. I suspect that every dollar spent by the client in therapy or coaching will save two—or more—dollars in the divorce proceeding. Why? Clients who are taking care of their emotional needs in therapy or coaching tend to need less contact and reassurance from me (which means I spend less billable time on their files) and do not run up fees in the legal process with aggressive, or passive-aggressive, attempts to meet emotional needs.

We'll talk in more detail about the emotional components of divorce in a later chapter, but note that seeking guidance and professional support from either a psychotherapist, counselor, or divorce coach early and regularly throughout your divorce is recommended and can help keep the cost of the process down. Support, in whatever professional package it comes in, is critical in this often difficult season of your life.

As you may already know, divorce can be one of the most stressful experiences of your life. This compounds an already challenging situation with exasperation or a scattered sense of "What now?" You can most easily get through this emotional turmoil by creating a working list that you can refer back to, both as an anchor and as a guide to help keep you moving forward. A list of the basic tasks will provide clarity for you to either complete the task yourself, delegate it, or easily identify that it's not one you'll need to complete.

As such, here is a starting point of a check-list (though you may adjust this, depending on your unique situation) that you can refer to as you move into this process:

- DIY—Is your divorce relatively simple and amicable? If so, you may be able to complete the divorce paperwork yourself. If you choose to do so, do you want to hire an attorney to review the paperwork to make sure that everything is in order? If you don't feel comfortable drafting the paperwork, is there an attorney who would do so, as an unbundled legal service?

- Legal assistance—If you need representation, but cannot afford it, what free or reduced-cost options are available to you in your jurisdiction?

- Compile a list of attorneys to interview—If possible, get several referrals. If word-of-mouth referrals aren't available, do some due diligence online and read up on attorneys in your jurisdiction. Make a list of your prospective attorneys and find out if they will do a free, or low cost, initial consultation, so that you may interview them.

- The attorney interview—Make a running list of questions to ask the attorneys. As we discussed earlier, you'll need to ask the attorneys questions about their backgrounds, practices, and experience levels. You should also make a list of questions you have about your situation. Remember that who you choose to be your attorney needs to be someone you're fundamentally at ease with (despite the circumstances), and with whom you feel comfortable bearing your truth. You're heading into a tough transition, and you need to feel supported and heard by your attorney, just as you would need to feel with a doctor.

- In addition to keeping a running list of questions, you'll need to find clarity around your finances and determine whether you can afford an attorney. If you choose to hire an attorney, you need to decide how you're going to pay for their fees. If you have to borrow funds to pay for fees, can these funds be repaid in a relatively short amount of time, with repayment terms that are manageable?

- Hire a divorce coach or therapist to get additional support so your emotions don't get played out in the legal process.

The Kids

Are My Kids Going to Be Okay if We Get Divorced?

The number one question most clients have at the initial meeting with me is "Are my kids going to be okay if we get divorced?" What I tell them is that the research is pretty clear. Your kids will be changed as a result of the divorce. Divorce is a big deal to them. Children feel deep pain from losing their intact, nuclear families, and they will be angry, disappointed, and sad. Additionally, the research shows that the effects of divorce on children are long-lasting and profound.

I also tell my clients that many researchers believe that sustained, serious marital conflict is even more damaging to children than divorce.

In short, whether the kids will be "okay" has a lot to do with how my clients and their spouses support the children during and after the divorce. There are many ways parents can promote their children's resilience, so let's talk about some of the key components for supporting your kids through this transition.

When and How to Tell the Kids

Almost invariably, my clients also want to know: "How and when do we tell the children about our divorce?"

Well, there is no right answer. A lot depends upon the children's ages and developmental needs. For example, you would not give the same explanation to a six-year-old that you give to a sixteen-year-old. That said, there are some general guidelines to follow.

First, withholding information from the children and not saying anything, is not a good idea. Kids pick up on things, whether they consciously know it or not. Leaving the child to figure out the status of her parents' marriage when one of you moves out is flat-out traumatizing.

Instead, both parents should be present to have this discussion with the children *before* one of you moves out. As parents, you should also have a "game plan" and be on the same page with how and what you are going to say to the kids before you sit down with them.

Many divorcing parents choose to tell their children that they are still going to be a family, but one that has two homes—one where Mom lives with the kids and one where Dad lives with the kids. Children tend to feel more secure when they know some of the technical details, like where Mom and Dad are going to be living separately, when they will get to see each parent, and where the dog is going to be. To the extent that you may know these details, share them with your kids.

Kids also often want to know why their parents are getting divorced. This may be the hardest part of the conversation, especially if one of you doesn't want the divorce or feels betrayed by the other. Regardless, don't overshare with your kids about your marital difficulties and don't blame each other. Less is more. Many couples opt for the "Mommy and Daddy love you, we care for each other, and we are all still going to be a family, but Mommy and Daddy cannot live together anymore" explanation, and it's usually enough to quell an anxious little heart.

Your kids will likely have intense emotions about this, depending on their ages, and your job is to keep calm during the conversation and not mirror your children's reactions. Mom and Dad need to be available to be emotionally supportive of the kids, regardless of the children's responses.

The children may have questions or simply want to avoid the topic altogether and end the conversation as soon as possible. If your kids do ask questions, answer them honestly and simply. Here, again, less is more. If your kids need space and time to process, give it to them.

Some psychologists also feel it is important to let third parties who are important in the lives of the children (for example day care providers, teachers, coaches, and parents of friends) know about the impending divorce. This way, the children can get extra support. Teachers and caregivers can be on the lookout for any change in the children's behavior. It is not unusual for children to have changes in behavior at school or drops in their grade point averages when they learn of, and begin to process, their parents' divorce.

Of course, not every divorcing couple adheres to these guidelines. Over the years, I have had many phone calls from clients who are reeling (or from opposing attorneys whose clients are reeling) after one parent separately tells the children about the divorce—usually with lots of drama, blame, resentment, and few—if any—facts about what the plan is or what comes next. While this is a real disservice to the children, there are things you can do to mitigate this circumstance.

First, do not use your spouse's poor judgment as an open door through which you can now relate your "side of the story" to your kids. Stick to the high ground and follow the guidelines outlined in this section (as well as the discussion that follows concerning "what" to tell the kids) when you speak with the children about the divorce.

Your kids may need some emotional support on top of what you and your spouse can provide. In other words, your kids may need some counseling to help them process the divorce.

What to Tell the Kids

Your kids need to know three things: 1) that each parent loves them; 2) that they did not cause the divorce; and 3) when and where they're going to be parented by each parent. That's it.

Many parents have the urge to overshare with their children. In fact, I would say the majority of my clients either want to defend their decision to get divorced, or blame the other parent for choosing the divorce. Do not do this to your children. TMI.

Oversharing with children inundates them with information that they are ill-equipped to process. It also creates a loyalty bind.

A loyalty bind is formed whenever children are placed in the middle of their parents' conflict. This hurts children and makes them feel uncomfortable loving both parents. In the long term, well after the divorce is concluded, this can tend to shape children into adults who avoid conflict and commitment.

If you don't want to be the reason your kid is in therapy as an adult, don't overshare with your kids and create loyalty binds that make them wrong for loving both you and your spouse.

Support and Nurture Your Children's Relationship with the Other Parent

Your children, whether biological or adopted, have been deeply imprinted by you and your spouse. They identify with each of you. And, if you have biological children, they were quite literally created with equal amounts of DNA from both you and your spouse. Kids know this intuitively, too. They get that they have a part of each parent in them.

It is not uncommon for a parent who is getting divorced to put down the other parent either directly to, or within earshot of, the children. When I hear about this happening in any of my cases, I cringe. I explain to my client that most psychologists would agree that putting down one parent in the presence of the child also puts down the child. Why? The child internalizes the insult because he knows that other parent is a part of him. In other words, kids feel that whatever is "wrong" about the other parent is also "wrong" with them.

Rather than criticize your spouse and attempt to restrict his or her access to the children, the best course of action is to nurture and support your children's relationship with your spouse. This is true (and can be especially hard) when the divorce has prompted your spouse to become a more active parent—maybe for the first time in your kids' lives. This may feel very insincere to you ("Why now?"), but if your spouse is well-meaning, it may be a very good development for your children.

So . . . just how do you nurture and support your kids' relationship with the other parent? Here are a few simple suggestions.

- For starters, you can *say nice things about the other parent* in front of your kids. Make sure your kids understand that parenting time with your spouse is important. Show them this by getting them to parenting time with their other parent *on time*.

- *Be positive* about the time the kids spend with your spouse.

- *Be flexible* about negotiating changes to the parenting time schedule to promote your children's relationship with your spouse.

- Finally, instead of taking sides or being the mediator between your kids and your spouse, *encourage your kids* to work out their differences with the other parent directly.

Do Not Put Your Kids in the Middle

Earlier, I introduced the concept of loyalty binds. To recap, loyalty binds are created when children are placed in the middle of the conflict between their parents. This results in the children feeling uncomfortable for loving each parent.

Occasionally, some parents intentionally create loyalty binds as a means of "winning over" the child. In my experience, these parents also tend to have serious mental health issues.

More commonly, at least in my practice, I see parents who *unintentionally* create loyalty binds by placing their children in the middle of parental conflicts through repeated—almost automatic—dysfunctional patterns that the parents engaged in during their marriage.

For example, arguing with your spouse in front of your kids literally places the children in the middle of the conflict. Don't do it—either during or after your divorce—even if you argued in front of the kids throughout your marriage.

Kids never become accustomed to having a front row seat to an embittered dispute between their parents. It makes them feel uncomfortable (even if they're unwilling to share this with you), and they don't want to see their parents interact in this way. Save your disagreements with your spouse for when your children are not present. If you don't have the opportunity to speak to your spouse (face-to-face or over the phone) without your children present, then address the issues through written communication (email, text) to which your children *do not* have access.

Divorcing parents should also be wary of putting the children in the middle by asking them to be a go-between. This can happen, for instance, if one parent tries to negotiate changes in parenting time through the child. ("Ask Mom if it's okay for me to pick you up on Friday at 7:00 p.m. instead of 6:00 p.m.") This also happens when one parent makes the child a messenger by giving the child something to take to the other parent, like a bill or a paycheck stub. ("Can you please give this to Daddy when you see him?") Even if you cloak the item in a manila envelope, your child will still feel like the intermediary.

Don't do this to your kids. Instead, keep them out of the middle by negotiating changes to the parenting time schedule directly with your spouse and by delivering a requested item yourself or through your respective attorneys.

When Does the Child Get to Decide?

Many clients who have children often ask me: "When is the child old enough to decide with whom he wants to live?" The answer is that the children usually do not get to decide this issue by themselves.

Rather, the children's preference, or opinion, is one of several factors that help determine the proper custody and parenting time arrangement. (See First *S*: Schedules in chapter 5.) Most states require that these factors (generally known as the *best interest standard*) be considered collectively, without one factor having sole responsibility for the outcome. As children age, however, their preferences tend to be given more consideration. In some states, the preference of a teenage child even becomes a rebuttable presumption regarding custodial placement. Why? Because children in their teens often have definite opinions as to where they want to be and when. As they're much more mobile by this point, they tend to choose with their feet (or cars)!

Generally speaking, though, with whom a child lives (usually called *physical custody*), as well as parenting time schedules, are decisions made by the parents with consideration for the children's ages, developmental needs, temperaments, and preferences. In the unlikely event that the parents cannot come to an agreement on these issues, the decisions are made by an arbitrator or by the court after some sort of evaluation or recommendation as to what is in the best interests of the children.

There is no doubt that divorce is a difficult transition for kids. Whether the "kids will be okay" starts and ends with how their parents choose to interact with each other, as well as with the children, during and after the divorce. The bottom line is *kids need to feel loved and supported by both parents*. Parents place their children in the best possible position to do well in divorce when the divorce is undertaken in a way that keeps the children's needs for love and support—from both of you—paramount.

Here are a few questions I would like you to introspectively consider as you navigate this rocky terrain. (If necessary, consult with your coach, counselor, attorney, or your spouse in order to get your perspectives in alignment.)

1. What do I need to do in order to be ready to discuss this topic with the children and my spouse?

2. What information can my spouse and I agree on to tell the children, and how will we do that?

3. Do my children and I need additional emotional support during this time? If so, what resources are available to our family?

These questions are merely meant to be a starting point for you to consider. For more information on this topic, please see *What About the Kids? Raising Children Before, During, and After Divorce* by Judith Wallerstein and Sandra Blakeslee.

The Legal Divorce

Divorce Laws Vary by State

Before we get started, I want to make sure you once again understand that the information presented in this chapter relates to *general* legal principles and concepts related to divorce. Please *do not* mistake this for *legal* advice in the state in which you reside. Each state has its own set of laws with respect to divorce. While there is certainly some uniformity to the legal principles involved in divorce, I strongly suggest that you meet with a divorce attorney licensed to practice law in the state in which you reside so that you can learn how the divorce laws in your state will apply to your own factual circumstances.

The Three *S*'s of Divorce

Generally speaking, the legal issues in divorce can be summed up by the three *S*'s—schedules, support, and stuff (a very technical, legal term!). *Schedules* pertains to custody arrangements and parenting time schedules. *Support* relates to both child support and spousal support (usually referred to as maintenance or alimony). *Stuff* is my catchall for your property, including your assets and your debts.

First *S*: Schedules

If you and your spouse have children, you two will have to decide who parents the kids when and what to call the arrangement. The time either parent spends with the children is commonly known as *parenting time* or *visitation*. (For our purposes, we are going to refer to this as parenting time.) You will probably also have to label your parenting arrangement, to determine with whom the children are going to live (*physical custody*), as well as who is going make the decisions regarding the children's health care, education, and religious training (*legal custody*). Custody (whether physical or legal) can be vested in one parent (*sole*) or both parents (*joint*). We'll talk more about all this in just a minute.

BEST INTERESTS STANDARD

Before we go further, though, you need to know that in most states the guiding principle in fashioning both custody and parenting time is the *best interests standard*. That is to say, the custody and parenting time arrangements must be in the best interests of the minor children. The vast majority of parents are able to resolve this issue, either on their own or with help (from their attorneys, a child specialist, or a mediator). They know what's in their children's best interests and are able to figure out the custody labels and parenting time schedules. And, generally speaking, the court will not second-guess the parents, as long as the arrangement appears to be in the best interests of the children.

For those parents who cannot seem to agree on custody or parenting time, a third party (such as a custody evaluator or judge) will help determine what's best for the kids. Regardless of whether the parties have agreed on custody and parenting time, or someone else is deciding this issue for them, the same yardstick is used, namely the best interests standard.

The best interests standard is normally defined by state statute, and often includes many of the following components:

- the wishes of the child's parent or parents as to custody;

- the reasonable preference of the child, if the court deems the child to be of sufficient age to express a preference;

- the child's primary caretaker;

- the intimacy of the relationship between each parent and the child;

- employment of each parent and the responsibilities of that employment;

- whether one parent may be unfit to parent;

- the interaction and interrelationship of the child with a parent or parents, sibling, and any other person who may significantly affect the child's best interests;

- the child's adjustment to home, school, and community;

- the length of time the child has lived in a stable, satisfactory environment, and the desirability of maintaining continuity;

- the permanence as a family unit, of the existing or proposed custodial home;

- the mental and physical health of all individuals involved;

- the capacity and disposition of the parties to give the child love, affection, and guidance, and to continue educating and raising the child in the child's culture and religion or creed, if any;

- the child's cultural background;

- the effect on the child if there has been abuse, whether the abuse was directed between the parents, between parent and child, or otherwise;

- the disposition of each parent to encourage and permit frequent and continuing contact by the other parent with the child.

In addition to these factors, some states have additional criteria used to consider requests for joint legal and/or joint physical custody. These can include:

- the ability of parents to cooperate in the rearing of their children;

- whether the parents have methods for resolving disputes regarding any major decision concerning the life of the child, and the parents' willingness to use these methods;

- whether it would be detrimental to the child if one parent were to have sole authority over the child's upbringing; and

- whether domestic abuse between the parties has occurred.

The weighing and balancing of all of these factors is something we'll discuss in greater detail in the section entitled Labeling the Parenting Arrangement.

PARENTING TIME

Parenting time falls into one of three types: 1) *regular* (who parents during the weekdays as well as on weekends, which can vary between the school year and the summer); 2) *holidays* (who parents the children on which holidays); and 3) *vacations* (how many days or weeks per year does each parent get to vacation with the children). Most of the time, holiday parenting time trumps vacation and regular parenting time, and vacation parenting time supersedes regular parenting time.

The amount of parenting time each parent gets with the kids varies wildly, depending upon the needs of the family. In most jurisdictions, though, each parent is encouraged to be actively involved in the parenting of the children, unless there are extenuating circumstances (like physical abuse, mental health issues, or chemical dependency). The idea behind this is that the input of both parents with respect to decision making and day-to-day caretaking is important in the rearing and development of the children.

In many families today, it is very common for both parents to work outside of the home and to be actively involved in raising the children. Some families, however, choose to have one primary parent stay at home with the children. During the divorce, it is generally a good idea, for the children's continuity and stability, to maintain a parenting arrangement similar to what they have known during their parents' marriage. Of course, this may not be entirely possible for a number of reasons. For example, it just might not be economically feasible for the divorcing parents to continue to keep one parent at home after the divorce.

Whatever the parenting schedule is, though, it is generally wise to put it in writing and incorporate it into the divorce paperwork. This is often called a *default schedule*. The default schedule usually specifies who parents when, and often references times for exchanging the kids. It can always be modified by mutual agreement between parents, as needs (yours and the kids) change over time. The default schedule is especially helpful for those parents who don't get along well, because it sets expectations as to when each parent will see the kids.

The other option, which some couples choose, is to simply grant one or both parents *reasonable and liberal parenting time* with the children. Again, what constitutes reasonable and liberal varies from family to family. With teenagers, the parents often designate one of their residences as primary (home base), and then the other parent sees the child at times convenient with the child's schedule. Sometimes, the parenting schedule can be coordinated directly between an older teenaged child and the parent. This works especially well with teenage children who are experimenting with increased freedom and responsibility. Often, teenagers are very involved in school-related activities, sports, or part-time employment. And, as most parents with teenagers know, when not involved in their activities, most teens prefer spending time with their friends, as opposed to their parents! So, flexibility is the name of the game with older kids. In these cases, the lack of certainty in a reasonable and liberal parenting time schedule can be appropriate, as opposed to a more rigid schedule with specific dates and times.

Two reminders about parenting time. First, it is good to remember that schedules tend to change over time as the needs of the children and the parents evolve. As children grow, they often need their parents to be more flexible to facilitate their expanded involvement in various activities, both curricular and extracurricular. Also, it is not unusual for divorce to stir things up for parents, too (spurring job changes, a health concern, or any number of other issues that might affect their ability to stick to a specific schedule). So, the number one buzzword with respect to parenting time is *flexibility*. That is to say, be adaptable to both your changing needs and your children's.

The second reminder I want to make about parenting time is that with the exception of older children—who need flexibility and who often want to give input toward the ongoing parenting time schedule—children generally do not want to be the referees of the parenting time schedule. Instead, children want Mom and Dad to figure out all the details and inform them about who is going to parent when. As we discussed in the previous chapter, asking children to decide when they see one parent or another sets up the children for a no-win loyalty bind that is bound to leave them feeling overwhelmed, uncomfortable, and stuck in the middle between their parents.

There is no one-size-fits-all approach to parenting time schedules. When trying to construct a schedule that is right for your kids, think about their temperaments and their developmental stages. (I have included in appendix C information about children's developmental stages and needs and how they relate to parenting time.) For example, a young, school-aged child who needs eleven hours of sleep a night should not have a parenting time transition at 9:30 p.m.! In the same vein, an infant needs consistent, reliable care from its primary caretaker in order to bond and form a healthy attachment. The infant also needs regular, consistent contact with the other parent, but which does not take the child away from the primary parent for long periods of time. Given this, equal parenting time schedules, especially a week-on, week-off type of arrangement, are not usually advisable for infants based on their developmental needs.

When creating the parenting time schedule, putting your kids' needs first is the top priority. Some parents find this hard to do since most of them want to spend as much time as possible with their kids. This is understandable, given that most parents feel very sad about having to now share the children and not seeing them every day. This is, however, one of the realities of divorce. It is the parents' job to work through their emotions around this issue and not compromise the children's needs and well-being by insisting on a schedule that does not suit the children's temperaments and developmental needs.

During divorce, some parents seek to expand their parenting of the kids (compared with their historical involvement). In many cases, this represents the well-intentioned desire to increase connection between the parent and the children. This is wonderful for the kids, although it tends to be very frustrating for the person who has historically been the children's primary parent. "Now, on the cusp of divorce, you're going to become an active parent and assert your two cents? What?" And yet, any child psychologist will tell you that a parent's authentic desire to increase—and sustain—parental involvement is generally a very good thing for kids, who reap the benefit of an enhanced relationship with the other parent.

Occasionally, however, requests to expand parenting time are misused as a way to reduce the amount of financial support one spouse may be ordered to pay the other. For the parents who are trying to increase parenting time so that they can decrease their financial support to the other parent (and then later disengage from the kids once the financial issues are resolved), I have one word: stop! Deal with financial issues head-on instead of playing games with your kids.

Determining whether the uptick in parental involvement is authentic or motivated by money is easier to figure out than you might think. The parent who honestly desires to increase his or her connection to the kids will state this desire and seek input from the other parent, as well as any professionals involved in the case (like the children's therapist or the child specialist), as to how to best accomplish this goal. In other words, the parent seeking additional involvement does not make a bunch of assumptions about what is best for the kids, and then make one-sided changes to the children's routine or schedules. The former is concerned about the kid's needs; the latter is concerned only about his or her needs. And that's the difference.

LABELING THE PARENTING ARRANGEMENT

In addition to determining the parenting time schedule, you and your spouse may also need to decide on what to call the arrangement.

Generally, there are two parenting arrangement threads that require labels. The first is the issue of physical custody, and the second is legal custody. Different states have different names for physical and legal custody. Sometimes the word *residence* is used for physical custody and *decision-making authority* for legal custody. Regardless of what they're called, the concepts of physical and legal custody are pretty standard.

Physical custody pertains to where the children reside and who is responsible, on a daily basis, for taking care of the children. Physical custody can be vested in one parent or both parents. If the children live primarily with one parent only, then that parent has *primary* or *sole* physical custody. If the children reside with both parents, then they will have *joint* or *shared* physical custody.

Legal custody pertains to the big decisions concerning the children, including their education, health care, and religious training. Like physical custody, legal custody can be assigned to one parent (*sole legal custody*) or both parents (*joint legal custody*).

Most states favor joint legal custody, unless there is a history of domestic abuse between the parents or other serious concerns about the parents' ability to share legal custody. Some states also have a preference in favor of joint physical custody. Regardless, the issue of custody (physical and legal) rises and falls on what is in the best interests of the minor children.

In some jurisdictions, the divorcing couple can opt to use a *parenting plan* instead of labeling their custodial arrangement. The use of a parenting plan focuses more on *how* the parties are going to approach and decide issues concerning their children. Some parenting plans can be very detailed and address all sorts of issues, including, for example, how each parent will introduce future partners to the children. Some parents opt out of this level of detail, but use the parenting plan to outline basic issues such as when each parent will have parenting time with the children, or what extracurricular sports and activities the children will participate in. Some parenting plan statutes (like the ones in Minnesota, where I practice) require the parents to label the legal and physical custody arrangement in the parenting plan! While at first blush this would seem to frustrate the purpose of using a parenting plan (that is, to get away from arguing about labels and focus on how to parent the children postdivorce), the statutes realize that the parenting plan may have to be interpreted by another jurisdiction (meaning a different state) that does not recognize parenting plans or that requires the identification (labeling) of the custody arrangement.

WHAT HAPPENS IF WE DON'T AGREE ON THE CUSTODY LABELS OR THE TERMS OF THE PARENTING PLAN?

Luckily, most parents do agree on the custodial arrangements or the terms of a parenting plan. Getting to an agreement can sometimes be difficult, but help is usually at the ready. And, if you truly cannot decide the issue, then there is a process for resolving the issue.

Conflicted parents sometimes use the help of a child psychologist (referred to as a child specialist in Collaborative Law) to help them come to an agreement on these issues. Parents can also use a process like the Social Early Neutral Evaluation (if available in your jurisdiction) or evaluative mediation to get feedback about what custody and parenting time arrangements might be best for their kids.

If, after getting mediation or additional help, you and your spouse are still at a crossroads, there is a process for resolving the dispute.

In most states, there would be some sort of objective review of the family system (called a *custody evaluation* or *study*), and the reviewer is usually a psychologist, social worker, guardian ad litem (a person appointed by the court to represent the best interests of the children), or a family law attorney. Once a custody evaluation is concluded, it often yields settlement. Why? Custody evaluations (especially those that are well researched and well written) are typically quite persuasive with the court.

The evaluation's focus is on the best interests of the minor child or children. It usually takes awhile to complete, because there are a lot of facts to gather. For example, the custody evaluator usually meets with both parents, in addition to the children, and may consult various *collateral contacts*, like the children's psychologists, teachers, and day care providers. The custody evaluator will also likely conduct home visits to witness the interaction between each parent when he or she is parenting the children.

The custody evaluator may also ask one or both parents to participate in chemical dependency evaluations or mental health diagnostic testing if the evaluator is concerned about the possible presence of either chemical dependency or a mental health issue. The evaluator also has access to psychological and medical records of the parties and their children. In addition, the evaluator often has access to the criminal and driver's license records of both parents.

When looking at the family, the evaluator wants to get a holistic picture of how the family functions, including the strengths and the challenges inherent both in the family's structure and its individual members. Only once the evaluator has a clear impression of the family can he or she analyze what would be in the children's best interests and make written recommendations.

These written recommendations are routinely called *custody evaluations* or *custody studies*. Most evaluations tend to look the same and have many of the same components. They usually begin with a presentation of the basic factual background of the case, and they include the contacts and information the evaluator has collected and reviewed. Since the facts provide the basis for the evaluator's recommendations, that data is almost always included in the first section of the evaluation.

The next section of the evaluation usually focuses on the analysis of the best interest standard, given the facts and circumstances of the case. As we discussed previously, the best interest standard is relatively uniform throughout the fifty states and includes several factors, all of which have to be analyzed, and then weighed against each other. This is not an easy task, and explains why it can take awhile (sixty to 120 days) for a custody evaluator to complete the study.

In weighing these factors, the evaluator may not generally use one factor to the exclusion of all the others. In most states, for example, this means that the evaluator may not solely determine the custodial arrangement based exclusively on the wishes of the minor child. That said, some states have decided that the child's preference should weigh heavily in determining custodial placement. In Georgia, for example, the preference of a child who is at least fourteen years of age is presumed to indicate what is in his best interests. In a different example, a child's primary caretaker cannot be granted sole physical custody without considering all the other best interest factors.

The evaluator usually draws up detailed written findings on each of the factors. He or she will also explain how the factors led to the report's conclusions and determination of the best interests of the child. The evaluator will also include whether he or she has (or has not) considered other factors or information outside of the best interests standard. Some states specify that evaluators and courts not consider conduct or evidence related to a proposed custodian if it does not affect the custodian's relationship to the child.

What does all this mean?

Say, perhaps, your soon-to-be ex has a boyfriend or girlfriend you can't stand, for whatever reason. And let's say that this person is also *never* around your children. Perhaps your spouse is dating this person only to meet imminent physical needs and has no intention of ever introducing him or her to the kids. If so, the new boyfriend or girlfriend may never be interviewed by the evaluator. Why not? If the new paramour is not going to be exposed to the children, and your ex does not plan to make the person a part of the children's proposed custodial home when the kids are with your ex, then the evaluator may simply not care.

Whether you like, love, or hate the custody evaluation, you are most likely stuck with its recommendations. This is because most trial courts see the evaluation as the "best evidence" of what is in the children's best interests. Most trial court judges feel that a decently prepared custody evaluation provides the best *objective* insight into the family unit. What's more, the court *expects* that one parent—and sometimes both—will not be happy with one or more of the evaluator's recommendations. Simply put, the evaluation removes the parents' dispute from the level of "he said, she said," and elevates it to a more objective, more rational plane, which is what the court prefers. In my experience, the trial court will adopt the recommendations contained within the evaluation approximately eight times out of ten.

In the two out of ten times the court does not adopt the recommendations of the evaluator, there may be problems with the evaluation itself, or the trial court may simply have a preference for a custodial arrangement that is different from the recommendations of the evaluator. Although rare, the evaluator may miss an important fact, may incorrectly apply the best interests standard, or may have had a clear, unsubstantiated bias in favor of one parent over the other. Judges have biases, too, and sometimes these filter (inappropriately) into their decisions.

If you are seriously disappointed with the custody evaluation and want to challenge its recommendations, the best approach is to retain your own expert to analyze the evaluation and provide a critique of it. This can be expensive, and it can sometimes be hard to make the expert look like anything other than a hired gun. Regardless, it is the only way to try and provide the court with an alternative that has any likelihood of success (as compared to trying to explain to the court, through your own testimony, why it should adopt your perspective over the evaluator's).

Luckily, as I mentioned earlier, the vast majority of cases do not need a custody evaluation—in most divorces, the parents are able to resolve this issue. This is wise. A custody evaluation can be very expensive—both financially and emotionally. In many jurisdictions, custody evaluations are conducted by private psychologists, social workers, and attorneys, who, as you know, charge for their time. As a reminder, the evaluator has to interview everyone, speak to collateral contacts, review records, and *then* write up the evaluation, which is usually quite detailed. The investment of this time results in a fee that can easily end up in the thousands of dollars.

In addition to the financial burden they create, custody evaluations can be quite emotionally costly. The evaluation draws out the conflict between the parents—for a long while—since an average custody evaluation can take months to complete. Sustained conflict is difficult for everybody. When speaking with my clients, I liken ongoing conflict to a boil on your behind. It's just plain uncomfortable! When you have a boil in a sensitive area, you know you have the boil, and the knowledge of this fact, coupled with tenderness and care required to attend it, are never far from the front of your mind. While it's there, you're always thinking about it, and it can make doing even the simplest of things, like sitting down, difficult.

Custody evaluations can also take you and your children out of your routines because the evaluation itself is invasive (think home visits, bringing the children to meet with the evaluator, getting records to the evaluator, and so on). It's like a part-time job, but not a fun one where you'd get discounts on cool clothes or free movie tickets.

Speaking of jobs, evaluations have a sneaky way of leading to difficulties at work and at school. Here, again, I credit the invasiveness of the evaluation, and the time and energy it takes to complete it. Unless you can add hours to your day, that time and energy has to come from someplace, and that place is often work (for you) and school (for the kids).

In addition, evaluations are hard on kids because they bring the children right into the middle of their parents' conflict. As I mentioned earlier, one of the factors in the best interest standard is the child's or children's preference regarding custody and parenting time. This puts kids exactly where they should not be—squarely in the middle between their parents. This often creates a loyalty bind for the child or children and hurt feelings all around.

There are, however, situations in which a custody evaluation may be unavoidable. These include cases where there are serious mental health issues or chemical dependency. In these cases, parents often are unable to put the needs of their children first, and so their circumstances drive the need for an evaluation.

Once custody and parenting time have been resolved, through either the parents' agreement or by decision of the court, the next issue to figure out is how to share the family's financial resources.

Second *S*: Support

The second *S* deals with two prongs related to the issue of financial support, including child support and spousal maintenance (otherwise interchangeably known as *alimony*). I will address each in turn, starting with child support.

CHILD SUPPORT

Child support is just that—money that is earmarked for the child's needs, such as clothing, food, and shelter. It does not usually include the many other costs associated with raising kids (like extracurricular activities, camps, music lessons, or sports gear), which have to be negotiated on top of child support.

Child support is often thought of as money one parent pays to the other to help support the kids. While it is true that sometimes a payment is exchanged between the parents, most state statutes look at the support of the children as both parents' responsibility. And most states have some sort of formula for figuring out how best to divide the expense of the children's support between the divorced parents. This division often results in payments from one spouse to the other to account for differences in either the parties' incomes or the amount of parenting time each party has with the children.

Sometimes the child support formula (often referred to as *guidelines* or *basic support*) does not adequately or fairly address the financial needs of the children. This may happen, for example, when a child has special needs and there are extra expenses associated with his or her upbringing. This also comes up when a child excels at something, say a particular sport, and there are additional costs associated with the child continuing to participate in the activity. There may also be instances in which the guidelines support is too high, given the circumstances, and may need to be reduced. In these cases, the parents—or the court—can choose to deviate from guidelines support. Whether upward or downward, a deviation usually requires specific fact-findings that reveal exactly how the adjustment serves the best interests of the minor children. This is because the law begins with the understanding that guidelines support amount is in the best interests of the minor children.

In addition to basic support, child support usually incorporates two other elements. These include the division of day care expenses (usually after the application of any tax credits) and medical expenses (premiums and uninsured expenses, like co-pays for office visits or medications), and different states have different ways of dividing these expenses.

Where I am licensed to practice, both the day care and the medical expenses are divided between the parties on a pro rata basis. This means that each parent contributes a percentage that reflects his or her share of the total combined income between them. For example, if the parents make a total combined income of $100,000 per year, and the wife makes $60,000 of that total, then she would contribute 60 percent (60,000 ÷ 100,000 = 60 %) toward the children's day care and medical expenses. The husband, who makes $40,000 per year, would contribute 40 percent toward the children's day care and medical expenses (40,000 ÷ 100,000 = 40 %). This kind of division is typically referred to as *income shares*, and has been adopted by many states.

Other states, like California and Alabama, typically split day care expenses equally between the parents. Some states, such as Texas, include day care expenses in the amount of total child support paid to the parent who has primary custody. Given the differences between states, it is important to research how your state allocates day care and medical expenses.

Most states do not consider extracurricular activities and expenses, like band or sports, to be part of child support. This is because the state prioritizes the child's *basic* expenses (food, shelter, and clothing) above the children's ability to participate in soccer or theater. If, after the provision of the children's basic expenses, the parties have some remaining disposable income, then the issues of which extracurricular expenses to fund, as well as how to divide extracurricular expenses between the parents, can be addressed. Some parents will choose to use relatively open language, such as equally sharing in all mutually agreed upon expenses, which only binds the parents to share the expenses on which they both agree.

I've seen other instances in which the parents choose to include much more detail, such as naming the specific expenses that they agree to divide, or specifically spelling out how the expenses are going to be paid when they are incurred. I think it is a good idea to include specific language if your children are already involved in extracurricular activities. You and your spouse may have to have some difficult discussions around this issue, because it is not always financially possible to support the kids' continuation in the same activities after the divorce.

If you and your spouse don't have the hard conversation during the divorce, you will likely end up having to determine which activities are mutually agreeable *after* the divorce. If you and your spouse aren't amicable, this can be a real minefield. Divorced parents often "agree to disagree" about the activities their children can participate in after the divorce is finalized.

Why? Well, first of all, many divorced parents have little extra money, and are simply unable to continue to fund a child's participation in a given activity. Also, some divorced parents may not want to agree to the time commitment and transportation requirements for activities that are scheduled during their parenting time.

If, on the other hand, your children are not yet participating in extracurricular activities, then about the only thing you can do is agree on how you and your spouse will divide up these expenses, when or if the expenses are incurred in the future.

In addition to child support and extracurricular expenses, there may be an issue of spousal maintenance, also known as alimony, in your case. The calculation of child support *does not necessarily precede* the calculation of spousal maintenance. They are frequently calculated at the same time because the child support formula may include the payment and receipt of spousal maintenance in the incomes of the payor and recipient, respectively. So, realize that the calculation of alimony may become integral to the calculation of child support and vice versa.

SPOUSAL MAINTENANCE

Spousal maintenance (or simply *maintenance*), which is sometimes referred to as alimony, is money paid from one spouse to the other from future income after the divorce. When the issue of maintenance is present in a divorce, it is often the most hotly contested issue in the case.

Why? Almost all prospective *maintenance obligors* (those who pay the alimony) do not understand why they have to share a portion of their future income (after the divorce), once the assets of the marriage have been divided. This is especially true when the spouse who is the prospective obligor is the spouse who does not want the divorce or who has been betrayed by his or her spouse. For these people, the idea of paying alimony adds insult to injury, and makes the whole process feel like they're being punished. In some states, however, an extramarital affair may mitigate the requirement to pay alimony. So it's important to research the particular laws in your home state or inquire about this in your initial consultation with a divorce attorney licensed to practice in your jurisdiction.

Regardless, the payment of spousal maintenance is not meant to be a form of punishment. It is meant to even out the divorcing parties' standards of living. It's often awarded when the divorcing couple has had a lengthy marriage in which one partner did not work outside the home or where there is a sizable difference in the current incomes, sometimes regardless of the length of the marriage. Courts generally see each partner's contributions to the marriage as important (even if they earned different amounts of money), and upon divorce, the court has the power to equitably divide income between the parties. Please note that I did not say "equally." Alimony is generally *not* seen as income equalization between a divorcing couple. Instead, it is seen as a contribution from one spouse to the other person's *reasonable* monthly expenses. (We'll talk about what constitutes "reasonable" in a minute.)

In sorting out the issue of alimony, the first step is determining whether there is even a need for it. Often, there is not. In this day and age, both partners tend to work outside of the home, and many earn enough money to be self-supporting—which renders the issue of alimony moot. If, however, there is a need for maintenance (meaning one spouse cannot self-support on his or her earnings alone), then the next question becomes whether the other spouse has the means to provide financial assistance. In many instances, the means are just not there. And if this is the case, the spousal maintenance analysis stops, and no alimony is ordered.

If there are both a need and an ability to pay, then the issue of alimony often moves along to a discussion of *term* (how long will alimony be paid and what are we going to call it) and *amount* (how much money is going to be exchanged between the spouses).

Generally speaking, there are three overall types of alimony, and they're designed to meet three distinct and different needs.

The first type of alimony is what is known as *transitional maintenance*. This type of maintenance is designed to provide financial assistance both during the divorce process and up to twenty-four months after the date of divorce.

The second type of alimony is known as *temporary* or *rehabilitative maintenance*. In some states, temporary maintenance incorporates transitional maintenance. The idea with temporary maintenance is to provide an amount of spousal maintenance for a limited period of time to assist the recipient-spouse in getting back into the job market or in seeking a higher paying job. Temporary alimony is also used to support a period of retraining for the recipient-spouse. I have had many clients who needed to update their teaching or real estate licenses or finish a degree program to be more marketable at a higher wage. Temporary alimony is designed to provide financial assistance during this period.

Temporary maintenance is not applicable in all circumstances. There are some cases in which the recipient-spouse will never become self-supporting. This could be as a result of some sort of physical or mental limitation, or simply because the recipient-spouse is older and has been out of the workforce for so long that they're not capable of self-support, even with retraining. In these instances, alimony may go on indefinitely. Again, different states have different names for this type of maintenance, including *long-term* or *permanent spousal maintenance*.

I know what you're thinking: "Just how long does permanent spousal maintenance continue?" That's a great question. There is no cookie-cutter approach to this answer, but permanent spousal maintenance generally is reduced or ends when there is a substantial change in the financial circumstances of either party. What this means is that one person—the obligor or the recipient—has had a marked increase or decrease in the amount of his or her earnings or monthly expenses. This often occurs at retirement, and I typically see requests for the termination of spousal maintenance obligations at this time.

Permanent spousal maintenance may also have a compensation aspect to it. This means that it reimburses the spouse who stayed out of the workforce, or worked a lesser paying job, often to facilitate child rearing or the other party's career advancement.

The issue of what to call the maintenance can raise considerable irritation among the divorcing couple because there is often a difference of opinion as to whether, or how quickly, the recipient-spouse should be able to become self-supporting. Also, the characterization of alimony may carry with it different presumptions about whether or how quickly the recipient-spouse is required to become self-supporting.

A recipient of transitional or temporary alimony may be expected to be self-supporting by the end of the term of maintenance. (A recipient of permanent spousal maintenance, on the other hand, may not have this same requirement.) So, once money runs out for the person receiving temporary maintenance, he or she may have great difficulty (or no possibility) of extending the length of maintenance. In contrast, the recipient of permanent spousal maintenance may have no requirement to ever become self-supporting. The thought behind this is that the recipient-spouse will be unable to recoup the foregone earnings and benefits lost over the several years (or decades) that he or she has been out of the workforce. This is the compensation component to permanent maintenance.

AMOUNT OF MAINTENANCE

In addition to the term or duration of alimony or spousal maintenance, the amount to be paid must also be determined.

This issue is never an easy one. In most cases, there is not enough income to meet both parties' needs at the former marital standard of living. For many couples, the concept of limited resources pushes them right into the fight or flight stress response, which we'll go into in more detail in the next chapter. When this occurs, it's not uncommon for each person to dig in and fight over every dollar. In a way, it can seem like each person is vying for his or her financial life.

With help, many divorcing couples can stay in a place of openness and creativity when it comes to maintenance. Why are creativity and openness important in determining alimony? Because there are lots of options for resolving this issue, but these options cannot be compared and evaluated if you're shut down due to the stress response.

In considering the options for spousal maintenance, we will first have to take a look at the incomes and budgets for both of you. Budgets often initially start out at the historical marital standard of living. This usually does not last too long, though, because in most cases, there is not enough money for each person to live—separately—at the marital standard of living. So, budgets have to be retooled to reflect what the new expenses are (if you have already separated) or what the budgets are likely to be (if you have yet to separate).

As you can imagine, people can argue long and hard over the reasonableness (or lack thereof) of each other's monthly expenses! I commonly see people argue over discretionary expenses, such as how much money each gets to allocate for retirement, travel, counseling, or eating out. I think the discretionary expenses raise the ire, especially in the spouse who is asked to pay maintenance, because the thought (of the obligor) is, "I will help you meet your basic monthly needs (like rent, food, and heat), but anything extra is your responsibility." This thinking, however, is faulty when compared to most state statutes, which take into account, in some reasonable manner, the couple's historical spending priorities during marriage, above and beyond the basics.

For example, I had a client who had been a stay-at-home mom for most of her marriage, and who had just recently reentered the workforce as a bank teller. Her spouse was a professional with a decent six-figure income. Historically, they had allocated significant portions of his income into retirement investments. On a go-forward basis (postdivorce), she had proposed continued retirement funding at reduced (when compared to the marital standard), yet substantial levels. Her husband was fine with funding his own retirement at this elevated rate, but not hers, postdivorce. His perspective was, "Hey, you're getting half the retirement, which is substantial, and part of my income to help meet your reasonable financial needs. Your 'reasonable' needs no longer include elevated retirement contributions." But her perspective differed. She believed that her elevated retirement funding was a very reasonable expense, given the precedent established during their marriage, and also given the fact that she was getting only half of their retirement funds and needed to earmark extra dollars to help replenish the retirement monies that were going to her husband. Ultimately, they agreed to an increased level of retirement savings for the wife, but not quite at the rate of savings that the couple had maintained during the marriage.

Most divorcing individuals, much like these folks, end up compromising on budgetary issues. And for many couples, the budget issues often sort themselves out, because there is only so much money to go around. The *estimated* budgets then become tailored to reflect the *actual* monthly income each person has, which will usually entail some difficult decisions as to where and how to cut spending and increase income. Remember, most couples are trying to figure out how to run two households on an income that used to service only one household, which is neither fun nor easy!

If there is enough money to meet both budgets, the analysis of "need" goes like this. The need is measured as the difference between the recipient-spouse's budget and income (whether actual or assumed). This difference is a net number, however, which has to be *grossed up* (increased) to account for the fact that the recipient-spouse must pay income taxes on the spousal maintenance received. In other words, the alimony amount to be paid would be the deficit between the recipient-spouse's budget and income *plus* the income taxes to be paid by the recipient-spouse.

Whether the spouse paying alimony (obligor) has a huge surplus of money left over every month (above and beyond his or her own budget) is of no concern to the recipient-spouse, as long as the recipient-spouse's budget is also met. Maintenance, as mentioned earlier, is not designed to equalize incomes between two divorcing individuals. It is seen as financial assistance from one person to the other for the purposes of meeting the recipient's reasonable monthly expenses.

How is spousal maintenance paid? Generally, alimony is paid in a monthly amount, in equal installments, synchronized with the obligor's pay periods. As an example, if your spouse is ordered to pay you the sum of $500 per month, and your spouse is paid bimonthly on the first and fifteenth of the month, then you will receive $250 on the first of the month, and another $250 on the fifteenth of the month.

Maintenance can be paid directly from one spouse to the other (via bank transfer or check) or through automatic income withholding, if your jurisdiction offers this service. So can child support. Automatic withholding can be really nice, because the payment comes directly from the employer to the state/county, which then forwards it to the recipient-spouse. If this service is available where you live, you should seriously consider it, even though a fee is often charged for participation.

Why? If you are the recipient-spouse, automatic income withholding is wonderful, because it virtually guarantees timely, regular payments if your spouse is a W-2 employee. An added benefit is that some states will automatically calculate and implement a cost-of-living adjustment from time to time. This is nice, because otherwise you would have to apply for this yourself. If you are the obligor, it is also a great service because there is no interaction between you and your ex. In addition, the state/county will keep a record of all payments made, so your ex can never accuse you of failing to make your payments.

Many jurisdictions also have the ability to apply pressure, in the form of driver's license suspension, to an obligor who has decided to shirk his or her child support or spousal maintenance obligations. They may also have the ability to perform *revenue recapture*, which allows the state to take the obligor's income or property tax refunds and apply them to any support or alimony payments that may have gone unpaid.

In addition to monthly spousal maintenance payments, you both may agree on—or the court may order—the sharing of bonus or commission income if the recipient-spouse's needs are not met by the monthly award of spousal support. In this situation, a percentage of bonus or commission income is awarded to the recipient-spouse, either net—after the payment of taxes by the obligor—or gross, so that the recipient-spouse has to pay the income taxes on the money.

This approach is often seen as the "fair" way to treat bonus and/or commission income, especially when this type of income is either speculative or paid out infrequently (quarterly or yearly). This way, the obligor is not obligated to pay spousal maintenance on income he or she may not earn. Even if the bonus or commission income is a regular source of income, it may not be paid out at the same interval as salaried income (that is quarterly versus monthly). Because of this variable, it usually isn't included in the monthly amount of spousal support. Otherwise, it could be a cash flow burden for the obligor, who might have an elevated monthly maintenance payment, based on income he or she isn't actually receiving on a monthly basis.

To illustrate this point, say that a husband has a consistent bonus income of $24,000 every year, which is paid out at the end of the year. And let's say that in the divorce, his ex-wife is awarded 50 percent of this bonus, gross (before taxes are withheld), when it is received. When the husband gets the bonus, his employer—or more typically, the husband himself—pays his ex-wife one-half of the bonus, or $12,000. The wife pays taxes on her portion, the husband pays taxes on his portion, and that's it. If, however, the wife's share of the bonus income had been included as part of her ex-husband's monthly obligation, then he would have had an additional $1,000 payment to his ex-wife every month (because her share of the bonus income is $12,000, which, divided by twelve calendar months is $1,000 per month). As you might imagine, this could be overly burdensome to the husband from a cash flow standpoint on a monthly basis.

As I mentioned earlier, spousal maintenance is taxable to the recipient-spouse, and deductible from the gross income of the obligor. This is a federal taxation rule, so it applies to all fifty states.

In order to avoid the issue of spousal maintenance altogether, some divorcing couples choose to handle it another way: they will agree to give whichever spouse is the "recipient" a greater share of the marital assets. The idea is that the recipient-spouse can then use this larger portion of assets to support him or herself, or to seek retraining. Some recipient-spouses save the additional assets, and either reduce their budgets to live on what they make, or they find better paying jobs to support their reasonable monthly expenses.

This kind of swap—an award of additional assets in lieu of spousal maintenance—is typically referred to as a *spousal maintenance buyout*, and it can be done in one of two ways.

Some couples want to completely eliminate the issue and consequences related to spousal maintenance—forever. Together with their attorneys, they often agree to a *sizable difference* in the amount of property each of them receives, with the recipient-spouse receiving *considerably* more.

Other couples prefer to have a fixed or short-term amount of spousal maintenance that will contractually end. In this circumstance, the agreement is that the recipient-spouse's willingness to receive a shorter term of maintenance is compensated by a larger share of the couple's marital assets. The amount of the spousal maintenance buyout is clearly less than a full buyout. This is because the obligor is also paying some amount of spousal maintenance for a period of time. So, receiving a period of spousal maintenance reduces the overall amount of the buyout.

In addition to cleaning up income tax issues and tying up the official loose ends between the former couple, a spousal maintenance buyout also has another alluring quality: it is not a taxable event. This means that the recipient-spouse does not have to pay taxes on the additional amount of marital assets received as a part of the buyout—although the obligor does not get a tax deduction in this scenario.

That said, the tax implications usually do get considered into calculating the amount of the buyout. This means that most buyouts reflect the consideration of the income tax implications to both parties. In addition, the spousal maintenance buyout is commonly reduced to represent the present value of a future income stream. "Huh?" you may think. The idea here is that if your spouse is buying out a maintenance obligation with property today, then there is a reduction based on an upfront payment. Why? Because a bird in the hand is worth two in the bush, as the old saying goes. If you're getting more property today in lieu of a payment stream over a period of years, then there is a discount for that security as well as the interest you could accumulate on the property over the period of years.

Spousal maintenance buyouts are to be considered *very carefully*. While receiving additional assets up front can seem extraordinarily appealing, the receipt of the assets usually closes—and locks—the door on any future spousal maintenance from the obligor. The inability to ever get spousal maintenance in the future, regardless of either party's circumstances, warrants serious consideration.

In calculating the amount and duration of spousal maintenance, some states require consideration of other factors, including whether there are children, the length of the marriage, and the amount of marital property acquired during the marriage. Other states, such as Colorado, use an online spousal maintenance calculator. In fact, some believe that a movement toward the use of a calculator is part of a larger, nationwide reform, in which many states are seeking to standardize spousal maintenance awards. The idea behind this interest in standardization is to promote consistency in spousal maintenance awards, which in turn, enhances the perception of fairness and predictability of the law.

The calculators vary, but in Colorado, for example, maintenance is determined by taking 40 percent of the higher income earner's monthly income and subtracting 50 percent of the lower earner's income. For example, if the higher earner's income is $100,000 per year, then 40 percent of this amount is $40,000. If the lower income earner's income is $50,000, then 50 percent of this amount is $25,000.

If $25,000 is subtracted from $40,000, this leaves a $15,000 per year deficit, which would amount to $1,250 per month ($15,000 ÷ 12 months = $1,250/month) to be awarded from the higher income earner to the lower income earner.

This amount, though, is intended only as an advisory guideline. The particular judicial officer assigned to the case still has a lot of discretion in determining the issue of spousal maintenance. Given this, it is important, if you are going to be dealing with the issue of spousal maintenance, that your attorney be (or get) very familiar with the spousal maintenance biases of the judicial officers in your jurisdiction. This is especially true if your case will be assigned to only one judge throughout your divorce. Why? Because having a good idea how your particular judge will rule on this issue will help expedite the resolution of the spousal maintenance issue—often without judicial intervention. If I know that Judge So-And-So does not favor long terms of alimony, then I can use this information in crafting, and responding to, offers of settlement in your case.

Now, let's revisit our previous example where we had one party making $100,000 per year and the other party making $50,000 per year. The guidelines for Colorado's spousal maintenance award pointed us to $1,250 per month. Now, let us presume that the party making $50,000 per year has a monthly deficit of $1,750 per month, while the other party meets his or her reasonable monthly expenses. It is possible that the judicial officer assigned to the case could grant an upward deviation to the guidelines to help reduce the monthly budget deficit of the spouse earning $50,000 per year.

Judicial discretion is necessary to avoid the occasional unfair spousal maintenance result, but I can tell you that it causes no small amount of worry among attorneys. Here's why: judicial discretion is not uniform. A few years ago in Denver, several metro-area judges were given the same fact sheet and asked to determine an appropriate spousal maintenance order.[1] The results varied wildly, from no spousal maintenance to $5,000 a month for life. The attorneys and judges alike were stunned. This mirrors my experience after close to two decades of practice in Minnesota. On the same fact scenario, one judge might award permanent spousal maintenance of $2,500 per month, but his judicial colleague right next door might award only temporary maintenance of $1,000 per month. This is why it so important for your attorney to know about judicial biases.

One final word about maintenance. As it can be one of the most controversial issues in any divorce, some prospective spousal maintenance recipients, especially women, can be pretty reluctant to assert well-grounded requests for alimony. In my experience, they are often afraid that requesting it will exponentially increase the conflict between them and their soon-to-be exes, and that doing so will draw out the divorce. I wish I could say that this fear is always unfounded, but that would be a lie. Raising a spousal maintenance claim does increase the conflict between the divorcing couple, as I have discussed. But so what? The issue of spousal maintenance is usually "closed" after the divorce is done, and there may be no possibility to come back later to request and receive maintenance if the recipient-spouse finds that he or she cannot self-support on the income or assets received as a part of the divorce. So, if the issue of maintenance exists in your case, even though it's likely to stir up tension, during the divorce is the time to deal with it.

Third *S*: Stuff

The next issue to be worked through is the allocation of marital property between the divorcing couple. In other words, how do we figure out who gets what?

PROPERTY SETTLEMENT

The first issue we have to address is whether you live in a community property state or an equitable property state. Most states follow equitable distribution. This means that in a divorce, the property acquired *during* the marriage will be divided between both of you in a fair and equitable manner. In these states, the focus is on weighing a variety of factors (such as the contribution of each spouse to the acquisition of the marital property, whether one spouse stayed at home to raise the couple's children, and the future earning potential of both parties) in deciding what it means for an award to be both "fair and equitable." To be clear, fair and equitable does not necessarily mean equal. While the divorcing couple (or the court) has the ability to make a disproportionate award to one party or the other, in my experience, the court often sticks to an equal, or close to equal, division of marital property, especially after a long-term marriage.

Community property states apply a different standard. Community property states currently include: Alaska (only by agreement), Arizona, California, Idaho, Louisiana, Nevada, New Mexico, Texas, Washington, and Wisconsin. In these states, spouses are deemed to *equally own* all income or assets earned or acquired during the marriage. This means that both spouses equally own the money (or income) earned during the marriage, even if only one spouse worked outside of the home. It also means that all property purchased or acquired during the marriage is owned equally by both parties, regardless of who purchased it. As such, in a divorce, all income and property acquired during the marriage are divided, usually equally. California, for example, mandates a strict fifty-fifty division of all community property. Other states are somewhat more lenient. For example, Texas laws allow for the "equitable distribution" of community property, which may result in an unequal division of property between the divorcing individuals.

Once you have determined whether you live in an equitable or community property state, then the process of figuring out the distribution of assets is pretty uniform. First, all marital assets must be identified. Marital assets include all real and personal property. *Real property* means real estate, including homes, cabins, time-shares, hunting property, farmland, and so on, whether owned in whole or in part by one or both individuals. Personal property includes all other property, including bank accounts, retirement accounts, investments, businesses, stocks, stock options, bonds, cars, collectibles, and household goods and furnishings.

In the process of identifying these assets, a question often comes up. Occasionally, a client wants to know if she has to disclose *all* the assets, even cash or other valuables, the existence of which she believes her spouse is none the wiser. The answer is: "Yes!"

First, no attorney with any integrity is going to partake in committing a fraud against the court by intentionally failing to disclose the existence of a marital asset. In addition, if the other spouse or attorney learns of the existence of the omitted asset, there could well be sanctions and the possible loss of any interest in the omitted asset by the nondisclosing party. Not to mention, you and your attorney will have zero credibility with your opposing spouse, his or her attorney, and the court. It is just not worth it. And what's more, assets are pretty easily traceable. We live in an electronic age where the Internet, bank statements, and credit card statements allow for the easy tracking of income and expenses. Even cash can be quite readily traced and added back into the marital balance sheet.

Once the assets have been identified, then they must be valued. With some assets, this is a straightforward proposition. For example, to value a bank account, all you need is a bank statement that shows the value of the account from the valuation date. (The valuation date is the date that the assets are valued. Often, the divorcing individuals will decide together upon the valuation date. If they do not, each jurisdiction usually has a default valuation date, like the date of separation or the date of the first regularly scheduled pretrial conference.)

If you own a business, for example, then the business may need to have a business valuation performed, if there is a disagreement as to its value. A business valuation is usually conducted by an accountant who specializes in business appraisals. The accountant will review and analyze the business's financial statements and lots of other information, and incorporate it all into a written report. In this document, the business appraiser ultimately comes up with an amount that usually represents the consideration of these three values: income approach (what the business is worth, based on its earnings), asset approach (what the business is worth based on its assets), and comparable sales approach (what other businesses like this one sell for in the open market). The value assigned to the business may also include certain discounting, or an upward deviation, depending upon factors such as whether the parties are the sole owners of the business or whether they are minority shareholders. Business valuations take time—often several months—and this can slow down the divorce considerably. What's more, business valuations can be expensive—easily anywhere from $5,000 to 10,000 or more—and paying for this expense can sometimes be a real burden (to the divorcing couple and to the business).

In a different example, a divorcing couple's home will often need to be appraised, which is much less time consuming and costly than having a business appraised. The parties will often agree on a neutral appraiser whose opinion of the home's value will bind both of them. (Sometimes there are good reasons not to have a neutral appraisal, but in my experience, they are generally few and far between.) The appraiser does an on-site visit of the homestead, and then assigns it a value based on an analysis of comparable sales in the area. The cost of the appraisal can vary wildly, from $200 to $1,000, depending upon the type of property and the experience of the appraiser.

Some people, though, either choose to bypass the appraisal of the real estate or simply do not have the money to pay for it. In these cases, the parties will often agree to use the tax value of the property as the value for the divorce. Other clients decide to determine value through one or more real estate market analyses (performed by a local realtor), usually at no cost. Sometimes one market analysis is sufficient. At other times, people will choose to get two or three market analyses and average them. Whatever works!

With regard to valuing retirement accounts and pensions, the valuation method depends upon whether the asset is a defined contribution plan, such as a 401(k) or a defined benefit plan, such as a pension. With a 401(k), all you need is the statement of value from at or near the valuation date. Since 401(k) statements are often generated quarterly, you may have to average values between the statement dates. Pensions are a bit more difficult to value, and usually need an actuary to determine the present value. Some people bypass valuing the pension by simply agreeing to divide it equally.

Other assets really do not need to be appraised unless the divorcing couple disagrees about their value. For example, most divorcing people appraise their own personal property. Even though it is important to them, household goods and furnishings are often valued at *what they could be sold for secondhand* (like through Craigslist or at a garage sale). Given this, I encourage my clients to amicably resolve this issue, since they could easily spend thousands of dollars appraising and arguing over assets that may be worth only hundreds of dollars—total. Other assets can be valued easily by the individuals themselves. I generally ask my clients to obtain the private party values for the vehicles through either Kelley Blue Book (kbb.com) or NADA (nada.com). Since the value of a car rises and falls based on the car's age, mileage, and option package, the client is usually in the best position to know this information, which is required to determine a value through either of these online resources.

Once the assets have been identified and valued, then they need to be allocated, or divided between the former couple.

And exactly how do assets get divided?

The assets are (usually) divided up based on the former couple's agreement. This happens about nine times out of ten. In the outlier case where the individuals do not agree, the court may need to intercede. But, beware! In my experience, the court is often inclined to just order the sale of the contested item of property. So, if you want to keep the item, it is best to negotiate some sort of trade or compromise for it.

When I work on allocating property between my clients, I start by creating a balance sheet (see appendix D) that identifies the asset, indicates its value, and details how that value was determined. I then have a column for nonmarital property (which we will discuss in a moment), and two columns for marital property—one for each spouse. In preparing the initial balance sheet, I start with the idea that the assets will be equally divided, and the balance sheet reflects my client's "wish list." That is to say, my client's one-half share reflects the assets they would most like to retain.

In the throes of a contested divorce, however, my clients do not always get a property settlement that reflects their "wish list." It is fairly common for both people to want the same asset(s), or for there not to be enough assets to divide in the way my client might prefer. Let's say my client may want to keep the homestead, and let's say the homestead has $100,000 of equity, and there are no minor children.

Let's also say that the homestead is the only asset of the marriage, and there are no retirement investments or savings accounts, which could offset the homestead's equity. While my client may want to keep the homestead, he may be unable to do so unless he can find a way to pay his ex her share of the equity in a timely fashion.

I understand that it can be hard for many of my clients to think about equally dividing their assets, especially if they were betrayed by their spouse or if they were the spouse responsible for earning or acquiring the assets. But remember that many states do not unevenly allocate assets based on marital misconduct.

This applies to the division of debt, too. Like assets, debt generally gets distributed equally or equitably between divorcing spouses. This can come as an unpleasant surprise—to put it mildly—to the person who did not incur, or agree to, the debt.

I've come across a few occasions where a client was completely unaware of a debt. For example, my client's spouse may have incurred gambling debts on a credit card that my client didn't even know existed, let alone the way in which it was being used. In this case, I may argue that my client's spouse should be solely responsible for the debt, and that it should come off of the marital balance sheet. The rationale is that my client should not be responsible for a debt he or she knew nothing about, especially one that may have been actively hidden by the other person.

Despite what you might think, the court does not always agree with this logic. Their reasoning is to not appear as if they are punishing one person for incurring debt (by awarding them the entire debt and removing it from the marital balance sheet), especially if an addiction (like gambling or drinking, for example) is present in the spouse who incurred the debt. It is not unusual for the court to include *all the debt* on the marital balance sheet and adhere to the idea that the debt is part of the "for better or for worse" arrangement that is marriage.

Now, a word about how the assets are divided. Sometimes this isn't a huge issue, because there isn't much to divide! If that's the case, then the hidden blessing is that there won't be much to argue about. If you have assets to be divided, then please know that they may not necessarily be taken, one by one, and equally (or equitably) divided, with each party keeping an equal (or equitable) interest in every asset. Instead, assets are often *offset*. What this looks like is that you might be awarded the $50,000 worth of retirement plans in your name, with your spouse getting the $50,000 worth of retirement plans in his name. Maybe you keep the homestead, and your spouse gets the cabin. Perhaps you take the JCPenney credit card debt, and he gets the debt to Home Depot. At the end of the day, you have to have an equal (or equitable) share of the assets and debts, and so does your spouse.

What happens, after offsetting the assets, if one person's share is substantially more than the other person's? Well, this situation generally needs to be balanced out by giving the other person more property or some sort of payment (I call it an *equalizer*), so that each has an equal (or equitable) share of marital assets and debts. In short, your attorneys will try to accommodate each of your wishes (to the extent that they're not conflicting). If this isn't possible, then we turn to mediation, mediation-arbitration, arbitration, or to the court for help. Most often (again, nine times out of ten), divorcing individuals will (eventually) agree on how to divide up their assets.

So far, we have discussed the identification, valuation, and allocation of marital property. But not all property is considered marital in nature. Often, one (or both!) of you have an interest in *nonmarital property*.

What Is Nonmarital Property?

Simply put, *nonmarital property* is property that is acquired by one spouse either prior to the marriage, or during the marriage in a particular fashion, most often through an inheritance or as a gift to only one spouse. When a gift or inheritance is made to one party from a third party (like a parent or grandparent), a nonmarital interest usually exists. Gifts between the individuals divorcing, however, are not considered nonmarital assets—with one notable exception in some states: the engagement ring.

In these states, the engagement ring becomes the nonmarital property of the wife upon the marriage. Why? Because the engagement ring is a *premarital consideration*, meaning that it is given in exchange for the woman's agreement to be married. If the marriage happens, the deal is sealed, and the ring becomes the wife's nonmarital property. (Since this varies by state, it is important to learn how your particular state will treat the engagement ring.)

In a divorce, a person's nonmarital property generally stays with them. So, if you received an inheritance of $25,000 from your great-aunt and kept it in a separate account in only your name, this asset should be awarded to you as your nonmarital property upon your divorce.

But here's where things can get messy. It is not unusual for people to take nonmarital monies (remember: inheritances, gifts, or bequests designated to one spouse only) and either commingle them with marital assets or place them in some sort of joint account or investment. When this happens, the person who wants to keep the nonmarital asset has to trace the asset and show what has become of it.

If the inheritance was used to buy a car, for example, and you want the car to be considered your nonmarital asset, then you are going to need to show the paper trail of how your inheritance became your car. So, you're tracing your inheritance, which has become *transmuted* into a new asset—namely the car. In this example, you might need to show estate planning documents (which awarded you the $25,000), your bank statements (showing where you deposited and withdrew the money), the cancelled check (the check you used to purchase the car), as well as the purchase agreement for the car in order to salvage your nonmarital interest.

What if you received the inheritance several years ago, and there is no paperwork to trace the monies? Well, all may not be lost. You may be able to prove the tracing through testimony. You would have to testify as to what happened to the inheritance. You would also need to provide as many supportive collateral sources as possible. For example, the personal representative of your great-aunt's estate may be able to testify as to the extent of your inheritance. Or perhaps, your sister accompanied you to the car dealership when you bought your new car (with your inheritance) and can offer testimony that corroborates your story. What's more, maybe the car dealership has paperwork from the sale of the car that could be introduced into evidence. All this, taken together, *may* be enough to show how your inheritance was transmuted and used to purchase the car.

If you are successful in demonstrating an asset to be nonmarital in nature, then that's it, right? Well, not exactly! Many states allow for the invasion of one spouse's nonmarital assets to avoid leaving the other spouse with nothing, especially after a longer-term marriage. In Minnesota, for example, one of the individuals in a divorce may request an award of up to one-half of the other person's nonmarital assets to avoid an "undue hardship" on the individual without the nonmarital assets.

Here's an example that might help show you what I mean: say that you and your husband have been married for twenty-five years. Throughout your marriage, you and your spouse have tended to spend what you earned, and have accumulated very few assets. Let's also suppose that two years ago, your spouse received a $500,000 inheritance from his mother. Now, you and your spouse decide to divorce. After twenty-five years of marriage, including three grown kids, a couple of job relocations, and a cancer scare, you have nothing to divide. If the nonmarital inheritance is awarded entirely to your spouse, you have nothing to move forward with in life after your divorce. It is in this kind of circumstance that some state courts will consider invading your spouse's nonmarital assets to give you an award to prevent the "undue hardship" of you leaving a long-term marriage with nothing while your spouse has $500,000. The amount of the award in this kind of scenario is often unpredictable, and is dependent upon the particular facts and circumstances of the case, as well as the prerogative of your judicial officer.

If you want to avoid the invasion of nonmarital assets, in addition to addressing other issues, such as the division of marital assets and liabilities and spousal maintenance (alimony), you may want to consider the use of a *prenuptial agreement* or *postnuptial agreement*. A prenuptial agreement (also known as an *antenuptial agreement*) is a contract signed by both of you prior to your marriage, and a postnuptial agreement is a contract signed by both of you after you've been married.

The use of pre- and postnuptial agreements is a relatively new development. Before the 1980s, such contracts, in the context of separation or divorce, were not enforceable and were seen as contrary to public policy. The thought was that they encouraged the contemplation of separation and divorce and would be used by the more powerful spouse to thwart an otherwise legal obligation to his or her spouse. Now, though, most states allow for the use of both pre- and postnuptial agreements, provided certain procedural requirements are met.

For example, one common procedural requirement is that the prenuptial agreement needs to be signed prior to the day of the wedding ceremony, and must be both witnessed and notarized. And many states require that in order for a *post*nuptial agreement to be valid, there must be no current contemplation of either separation or divorce for a period of time (which varies state by state) after the signing of the agreement.

A valid and enforceable prenuptial or postnuptial agreement can successfully limit—or prohibit—the division of certain marital and nonmarital assets. Most often, this happens when couples want to exclude previously acquired assets from becoming marital assets of the upcoming (prenuptial) or current (postnuptial) marriage. Further, the couple may also decide to use the document to control the division of assets acquired during the marriage.

I have also seen both pre- and postnuptial contracts that try to put restrictions on spousal maintenance (alimony) in the event of divorce. Sometimes this works, and sometimes it doesn't. In my experience, courts carefully scrutinize complete waivers to any and all future maintenance. This is especially true in cases where the marriage has been relatively long in duration, and also in cases where one spouse has left or forgone employment to raise young children. In these cases, the court can usually dispatch with the strict enforcement or application of an otherwise valid pre- or postnuptial contract to allow for a more equitable result.

In interpreting a pre- or postnuptial contract, the court generally has to make sure that it is fundamentally fair, both at the time the document was signed, and also at the time of divorce. It may be all well and good to have contemplated limiting spousal maintenance at the outset of the marriage when both spouses were gainfully employed and making similar incomes. But if, say, the couple is now divorcing after fifteen years of marriage, and the wife left a well-paying job ten years ago to become a stay-at-home mother, it may not prove to be so fair and equitable to the court, especially if her spouse has the financial ability to support both parties.

As you can see, unwrapping your and your soon-to-be ex-spouse's lives in the legal divorce can be quite complex, especially when you've been married for some time, have children together, and have acquired property. Because divorce is a painful experience, I see clients try and rush the process, hurrying through the discovery phase to "get it over with" faster. I'm here to slow you down and acknowledge the pain you may be experiencing, but also to remind you that this, too, shall pass. Unpacking your legal baggage is only one part of the puzzle, and often will move more swiftly if you also look at the other pieces of the dissolution pie, which we'll talk about shortly.

Before we move on, here are a few points of consideration about the legal aspects of divorce.

Have you put together a plan for what an ideal divorce resolution would look like? With regards to the three S's in the legal divorce, consider your best-case scenario, and sketch it out so you are ready to share and discuss it.

1. **SCHEDULES**: What's your ideal parenting time schedule regarding routine, summer, vacation, and holiday parenting time?

2. **SUPPORT**: How do you envision support (child support, spousal maintenance) between you and your ex? How are child support and spousal maintenance calculated in your state? What's your income? What's your budget? Do you have sufficient income to meet your monthly expenses? If not, does your spouse have the ability to assist you financially? How long might you need financial assistance? What's your plan for becoming self-supporting? If your income

exceeds your budget, is your spouse in need of financial support from you? If so, why and for how long? What's your spouse's plan to become self-supporting? What do you believe would be a reasonable term of maintenance and amount?

3. **AND LASTLY, STUFF:** Have you made an earnest inventory of all the property (both marital and nonmarital) and assets between you and your ex? If you were to fairly divide what you have between you, how would you propose doing so? Is there any nonmarital property that needs to be accounted for? Do you have a pre- or postnuptial contract? Are there any assets that will need to be appraised? Can you and your spouse agree on a neutral appraiser?

The Emotional Divorce

The Physiology of Emotions

Perhaps your spouse just told you that he wants a divorce. Your breathing quickens and becomes shallow. Your heart races and feels like it's beating out of your chest. Your palms begin to sweat. You want to bolt. You can't think of anything to say.

What the heck just happened? You had a stress response! An ancient part of your brain was stimulated in response to a perceived threat. Specifically, your sympathetic nervous system has been triggered. When this occurs, the body prepares to fight or flee the perceived danger. Blood is shunted into the large muscles. Respiration, blood pressure, and heart rate all increase. All nonessential bodily functions, including critical thinking, are shut down. Your perceptual field narrows, and your options appear to become fewer. Your adrenal glands secrete certain stress hormones, including adrenaline, cortisol, and epinephrine. Their roles are to make you more awake, aware, and focused, with the ability to react immediately. While processing the threat, you also experience *attentional blink*, in which your brain takes a short break from taking in information. So, you don't see what's happening around you, and you don't hear what someone is saying to you.

The sympathetic response works great if you have to run from a dog or fend off a brown bear that has wandered into your campsite! It is not your friend, though, if you are sitting in mediation with your spouse and your respective attorneys, and you become triggered by something your spouse says. Not only will you become physically uncomfortable, but you will also lose the ability to analyze and think critically. There will seem to be few, if any, options to consider. You may become increasingly aggressive, defensive, and protective, or you just may want to take off and sidle up to the nearest bar. Beneath all that, you will be driven to react quickly, all while taking in less information! Sounds like a recipe for disaster, doesn't it?

So, when is the stress response most likely to occur and how do we deal with it? The stress response is activated by mortal threats (to either yourself or to loved ones), physical pain, emotional upset, significant stress, significant excitement, or even low blood sugar. These things happen all the time in a divorce, and sometimes at the same time! Think about sitting in that mediation session. You are worried about where you and your kids are going to live after the divorce. Work has been busy, and one of your kids has been sick, so you've been under significant additional stress. You also stubbed your big toe on your left foot two days ago, and the nail has now turned blue and is throbbing. To top things off, you had three cups of coffee and a donut for breakfast—four hours ago. And now your spouse says that both you and your budget are crazy!

The stress response crops up all the time in the context of divorce. And not just in mediation or at a court appearance. It also happens in seemingly nonthreatening environments. For example, my clients have had stress responses while reviewing a counterproposal with me, or as a result of reading an upsetting text or an email from their spouses. Some people experience their divorces almost entirely from the perspective of their sympathetic nervous systems, while others are not so easily triggered.

No matter when or where it happens, once the sympathetic nervous system is triggered, there is no point in moving forward with discussing an issue or making decisions until the response has subsided. And just how is the stress response tapered? The answer is by shifting into your parasympathetic nervous system.

If you think of the sympathetic nervous system as the gas pedal, then the parasympathetic nervous system (PNS) is the brake pedal. The PNS is commonly referred to as rest and digest, because it promotes rest, relaxation, and digestion. The PNS may also lead women, primarily, to tend and befriend, that is, to calm their stress responses by taking care of their offspring and seeking relationships that offer social support.

Activating the PNS restores the functions of the neocortex of your brain, which are pretty important! These functions include: rational and critical thinking, seeing the big picture (perspective), foresight, problem solving, judgment, empathy, creativity, intuition, and insight, among others. All necessary and useful functions when contemplating and making important decisions in divorce.

So, how do we shift into the PNS? Rick Hanson, the author of *Buddha's Brain*, suggests the following techniques.

- Breathe from your diaphragm. This stimulates the PNS by slowing down your breathing. Put your hand on your stomach. If it rises up and down as you breathe, you're breathing from your diaphragm.

- Combine diaphragm breathing with mindfulness. Pay attention only to what is happening in the present moment. This will help you shift into the PNS, creating a feeling of calm and relaxation.

- Use imagery to stimulate the PNS. Visualize yourself in a peaceful place. It could be walking on the beach at sunset or walking a trail in the forest early in the morning. It is important to use all your senses in this imagery—sights, sounds, the feel of the sun or wind on your face.

- Lightly run one or two fingers over your lips. Parasympathetic fibers are spread throughout your lips, so touching them stimulates the parasympathetic nervous system. (Sounds weird, I know, but it works, and quickly!)[1]

You can calm yourself with these techniques, and also by taking a break from the action. In mediation, if my client has become triggered, I take a restroom break or say that I need to speak to my client alone. If I am working with my client at the office, I take a few minutes to talk to him about the stress response, as he often won't notice when it begins (as it's activated so much of the time in a divorce). We also tend to go off topic for a little while and talk about something completely unrelated to the issue at hand, like the weather or a sporting event. Many attorneys also keep food in their offices and conference rooms, like granola bars, chocolate, or trail mix, to promote the rest and digest functions of their clients' parasympathetic nervous systems.

Your body has a wisdom that is ancient, and which has kept you, and your ancestors long before you, alive. Your stress response serves you very well when you need to swerve quickly to avoid a deer on the highway or when you're running a competitive race. Your stress response, however, can undermine you in the throes of negotiating a resolution to your divorce. When you know how the stress response is triggered, and how to shift yourself back into the parasympathetic nervous system and the higher functions of the neocortex portion of your brain, you will be able to respond, and *not* react, to the situations and circumstances of your divorce.

Navigating the Pain

For many people, going through a divorce is one of the most painful events of their lives. When I ask my clients how they're doing emotionally while we're making our way through the legal process, I usually hear responses like, "Ugh, it's tough," or "It's so painful," or "I feel afraid and uncertain of the future," or "I don't know, actually, because I'm in such a fog right now."

What I don't generally hear is this: "Oh, I am so grateful for the process—and for everything, really—and all I'm learning!"

I hear you chuckling out there! I'm laughing a bit, too, because I can count on one hand the number of clients who have had this level of positivity, present moment awareness, and gratitude over the time I've been in practice. And yet, we all should be cultivating a practice of gratitude, because the research very clearly demonstrates the positive effects it holds for us.

The Research on Gratitude

Three leading researchers on the issue of gratitude include Dr. Robert A. Emmons (University of California, Davis), Dr. Michael E. McCullough (University of Miami), and Dr. Martin E. P. Seligman (University of Pennsylvania). In one research study conducted by Drs. Emmons and McCullough, those who wrote about gratitude were more optimistic and pleased with their lives than were other participants who wrote about irritations or events that had affected them.[2]

In a different study, Dr. Seligman found that participants had a substantial, immediate, and relatively long-term (a month in duration) uptick in their happiness scores from writing and personally delivering a letter of gratitude to someone who had never been properly thanked for their kindness.[3]

Gratitude has also been shown to affect stress and depression. In 2008, Alex M. Wood (Department of Psychology, University of Warwick, England) and his colleagues published the findings of two longitudinal studies, both of which showed that gratitude tended to "protect people from stress and depression."[4]

Perhaps not surprisingly, personal relationships are positively affected by the expression of gratitude. Gratitude in the context of relationship is more than just saying "Thanks for picking up the kids from soccer practice." It means being appreciative of who our partners are as human beings, and remembering their best traits (which is why we entered a relationship with them in the first place!).

Sara B. Algoe, from the University of North Carolina, and her research colleagues from the University of California (Santa Barbara and Los Angeles) found that couples who expressed gratitude felt closer to each other and were more satisfied in their relationships.[5] Dr. Amie M. Gordon (in research conducted through the University of California Berkeley) found that partners who felt gratitude toward their mates were more likely to stay in their relationships (over the following nine months). Why? Dr. Gordon suggests that gratitude fosters a cycle of generosity between partners, which in turn, helps relationships thrive.[6]

SO HOW DOES GRATITUDE RELATE TO DIVORCE?

The research on the effects of gratitude is pretty clear. Gratitude is associated with the enhancement of optimism, happiness, motivation, and satisfaction in relationships. It also appears to help reduce stress and depression.

How does this sound to you, especially if you're currently struggling with the pain and difficulty of divorce? If these benefits are enticing, are you willing to take a couple of small action steps to cultivate gratitude and help yourself feel better?

First, start a very simple, but daily, gratitude journal. It does not need to be an exhaustive list which only adds to the angst and stress related to an already busy life. Three things. That's it. Each can be one word (or more, if you like). Write out the list on your iPhone on the subway on the way home from work, or while you're waiting to pick up your children from school. It doesn't take more than twenty seconds, and we all can find twenty seconds to bolster our happiness while reducing stress and depression.

Look for new things to appreciate and add them to the list. Record the joyful things, certainly, but also give thanks for the difficulties in life, too. Why? The difficulties are the cracks in the veneer of our lives, which let the light in—to paraphrase Leonard Cohen. The light can help illuminate and shift our outdated perspectives and longstanding negative, self-limiting beliefs and patterns.

Painful experiences can also help remind us of the simple joys that we often overlook and take for granted. For example, watching my father (who has emphysema) struggle to breathe reminds me what an amazing gift it is to be able to take a deep breath.

The trials and tribulations of life also reveal our strength, courage, and resiliency. They assist us in developing character and depth. Dr. Elisabeth Kübler-Ross had this to say about how we can be tempered through life's difficulties:

> The most beautiful people we have known are those who have known defeat, known suffering, known struggle, known loss, and have found their way out of the depths. These persons have an appreciation, a sensitivity, and an understanding of life that fills them with compassion, gentleness, and a deep loving concern. Beautiful people do not just happen.[7]

In addition to keeping a daily gratitude journal, the second action step is to make a *one-time list* of three attributes of your spouse for which you are grateful. Yes, that's right. I am asking you to express gratitude for your spouse. It may be as simple as "He's a good dad," or "She can be funny," or "He goes to work every day." If you struggle with this action step, think back to the reasons you married your spouse in the first place. Your spouse's admirable traits, with which you presumably fell in love, are probably still there, even if you no longer experience them.

Once you create the list, reflect on it from time to time. It can be very helpful to review the list right before mediation or a meeting in which you have to interact with your spouse. Why? Remember, expressing gratitude helps reduce your levels of stress and depression, while elevating your happiness and optimism. So, use gratitude for your spouse as "a shot in the arm" before dealing with a stressful situation.

I will also tell you that I have seen miracles occur in divorce when one partner utters a few grateful words to their spouse, especially in the context of mediation or in a joint meeting involving both people and their attorneys. The words tended to soften the other party and seemed to assist in bridging what appeared to be an intractable impasse. Given these experiences, I personally believe that gratitude truly changes the energy of the room. It's as if the expression of kindness creates a portal that promotes and elevates each person's willingness to cooperate and collaborate.

Simply put, gratitude works. The research shows that being grateful can help us be happier, more optimistic and motivated, while simultaneously reducing levels of stress and depression. If there is any time in life when we need more happiness, optimism, motivation, and less stress and depression, it is while going through the process of divorce! Consider adopting a gratitude practice to enhance your own resilience during this difficult transition.

As an attorney, I help my clients navigate the legal elements of divorce. At its core, the legal divorce is a business transaction involving the negotiation and settlement of parenting time schedules, child support and spousal maintenance, as well as the division of assets and liabilities. The legal divorce is the how—that is, the mechanics of getting divorced. The emotional divorce, on the other hand, is the why, and it is, by far, the biggest, and most important, piece of the dissolution pie.

The legal divorce is relatively predictable. I can generally give my clients the lay of the legal landscape, which varies depending upon how agreeable the couple is. On one side of the fence is the green, verdant pasture of amicable settlement. On the other side is a stinky swamp, filled with the muck of long drawn-out litigation, pain, and animosity.

As you either know or can imagine, the aspects of emotional divorce are far more textured than the legal components of divorce. It is a process, to be sure, and I find that many people don't want to go through that process because of how painful it is. Also, this culture doesn't allow for much room to mourn anything. You might get a day off from work when you have to attend a funeral, but there is generally no understanding, whatsoever, of the need for time off to grieve the death of your marriage.

Over the years of teaching many divorce information seminars, on two separate occasions I had an attendee—who was currently facing divorce—open up about having previously lost a spouse to death. On both occasions, each attendee talked about how hard the divorce was in comparison to the death of their former spouse. With death, they said, there is a certain finality. You are not going to see your spouse at birthday parties, football games, and at the beginning and end of parenting time.

What's more, each attendee shared how much more empathy and sympathy they received when their spouse died, as opposed to when they went through their divorce. When their spouses died, their relatives, friends, and neighbors brought over food, offered to take care of the children, and invited the spouse in mourning to social events, like going out to dinner or to a movie. In contrast, relatives, friends, and neighbors tended to keep their distance from the divorcing spouse. Each attendee shared how much more alone they felt through the whole process of divorce as compared to the process of losing a spouse to death.

It's a Process: The Five Stages of Grief

Even though divorce does not usually result in the death of either party (!), the process for mourning the loss of the marriage has the same steps as mourning the loss of someone to death. The stages of mourning were pioneered by Dr. Elisabeth Kübler-Ross over forty years ago in her book *On Death and Dying*.[8]

Before we discuss the five stages, I want to mention a few important things you need to know about the grieving process. First, *grief does not follow a linear progression*. You do not complete one stage, and then neatly move on to the next. Grief is messy. Sometimes you take two steps forward, only to have a complete breakdown, after which you promptly take three steps backward.

In addition, you will grieve even if you instigated the divorce in the first place. Whether or not you want to be divorced, you still have to mourn the loss of the hopes and dreams you had for your marriage.

Everyone wants to know how long the grieving process takes. Although there are some who say that one year of grieving is needed for every ten years of marriage, in my experience, there is no cookie-cutter approach. Everyone has a different path through mourning. One of my friends was married for only six months before she divorced. She needed nearly three years to heal after her divorce and before she was ready to date again. Another friend was married for thirty-four years. Despite having divorced several years ago, she is now back in the stage of anger over a conflict she is having on a postdivorce issue. Some clients of mine have had a much quicker trajectory and have needed only a period of months—as opposed to years—to mourn, because they had started the grieving process while they were still married.

To this end, the process of grieving has five stages, including denial, anger, bargaining, depression, and acceptance.

Let's dive into each for a better understanding.

DENIAL

One of the definitions of denial is "the refusal to acknowledge the existence of something." In other words, "This isn't happening to me!" It can take a lot of forms, though I see two common patterns in my practice.

The first is the spouse who just does not believe that his or her spouse wants out of the marriage. The spouse in denial presses the "Ignore" button, and simply continues the marriage as usual. Even once their spouse moves out of the home (and sometimes in with another person), the spouse in denial believes that the separation is just temporary so that they can "work things out."

The other pattern of denial I commonly see is a spouse who fails to acknowledge a behavior, which has significantly contributed to ending the marriage. I have seen this happen with the alcoholic who does not believe his drinking is "any big deal," or the woman who has cheated on her husband, but who does not seem to understand why the indiscretion should be the basis for ending the marriage.

The most important thing to know about denial is that it is completely normal (as are all the other stages). Denial allows us to slowly grasp the facts of a situation, which would otherwise be overwhelming. Said differently, denial helps us deal with the pain in bite-size pieces by ignoring the totality of the circumstance . . . if only for a little while.

ANGER

Once we step out from behind the veil of denial and begin to see the picture of what is actually going on, then we are going to be mad. We might be angry at our spouse for betraying us with another person or with the bottle. We might be torqued that our spouse no longer wants to work on the marriage. We may be upset with ourselves for tolerating unacceptable behavior for far too long, or for not being loving enough toward our spouse. We may feel bitter about the effect the divorce is having on the children, or because we have less money since the separation. There are as many different reasons to be angry in divorce as there are divorcing people.

BARGAINING

Bargaining can be summed up as "rearranging the deck chairs on the Titanic." It comes up when we think about how we would have changed a situation in the past, or a current situation over which we have no control. When my clients rearrange the deck chairs, I will hear statements such as, "If only we had stayed in counseling longer," or, "I should have forced her to go to treatment." Bargaining is a form of Monday morning quarterbacking, and focuses on how the marriage, like the football game, could have been "won" if only we had been at the helm and called out different plays. Bargaining is a defense mechanism in which we alleviate feelings of hurt, helplessness, and vulnerability by trying to take back some amount of control.

DEPRESSION

This stage is characterized by deep sadness and hurt over the loss of the marriage. It is also characterized by fear—especially of the unknown.

Depression looks different on everybody. Some find it hard to get out of bed in the morning and face another day. Others struggle with insomnia. Some people put on weight; others can't keep meat on their bones. Often there is palpable sense of loneliness, coupled with a yearning for the "good times" with the ex. Many women, in particular, have nightmares about becoming a "bag lady" and living under a bridge. Almost everyone worries about what the future holds and how they are going to make it financially. Sometimes the fear is so overwhelming that it catapults the worrier back into the stages of denial, anger, and bargaining.

Depressed clients, or opposing spouses, can also play the blame game by labeling their spouse as a _____ (fill in the blank with "alcoholic," "pathological liar," "narcissist," "borderline," and the like). This is a way of dealing with the pain without accepting any responsibility for having helped create it.

ACCEPTANCE

There is a bit of grace in acceptance. It comes about when you surrender to what has happened, and acknowledge that the marriage, along with all your hopes and dreams for it, are gone.

With acceptance comes a feeling of peace. The volatile feelings surrounding the divorce, and your spouse, begin to subside. This looks like going to your child's soccer game and not having that pit in the middle of your stomach when you see your former spouse on the sidelines. It is regaining mindshare—meaning days, weeks, months—when you haven't thought about your divorce or what a jerk your ex was. It may also feel like readiness—to go on a date with someone new, or to look at all the possibilities in creating the next chapter of your life.

RESISTANCE COMPLICATES GRIEVING

There is an old saying that says what we resist, persists. In other words, what we don't want to acknowledge or feel usually ends up being served up raw for our review, again and again and again until we are willing to look at it and feel it. One divorce coach with whom I presented said it this way: resistance is like a high interest rate credit card. If you don't retire the balance, the interests just keeps compounding and compounding. Eventually, the interest will be more than the original debt.

Perhaps you have experienced this scenario. Have you met someone who described his divorce in exasperated terms, as if it had occurred last week, only to find out that the divorce was finalized ten years ago? This is complicated grief.

The antidote to complicated grief is simple, but not easy: mourn the death of the marriage and the loss of the dreams that were part of it. You may need a therapist to help you through the grieving process. You will also need time, unfettered by the feel-good pheromones and excitement that are typically part of a new relationship.

Taking Blame out of the Equation

We all do it, don't we? We blame. Sometimes we blame ourselves. Sometimes we blame others. There's a certain addictive quality to the righteousness—and the closure—both of which are part and parcel of blaming and faultfinding.

Blame is defined as assigning responsibility for a fault or a wrong. Blame can be directed at ourselves (self-blame) or focused on others. Believe it or not, blame is actually steeped in perfectionism, a poor self-esteem, and a willingness to judge.

Where perfectionism rules, blame festers. When mistakes are seen as "bad," there is guilt by association: the people who make mistakes are also "bad." When perfectionism is coupled with low self-esteem, a proclivity to judge is predictable, and a vicious cycle is born.

Perfectionism is an impossible standard-bearer . . . and a mighty taskmaster. It makes someone who already feels unworthy incapable of admitting a mistake. To a person living with perfectionism, admitting a mistake would even further destroy an already weakened self-esteem. So what happens?

The shame related to making a mistake is projected outwardly on to someone else, via judgment. Judgment, in turn, puffs up the blamer's self-worth by making them feel morally superior—somehow closer to that unattainable golden ring called perfection. This completes (and naturally restarts) the vicious cycle of blame.

If it isn't already obvious, blame is dangerous. Why? It is a cheap way of seemingly putting our problems to bed without really addressing or learning from them. In cases of self-blame, it helps us keep our faces squarely in the dirt. Blame confuses the deed with the doer. It makes the doer (whether the blame is placed on ourselves or on someone else) appear less worthy of respect. A lack of self-respect is what keeps people in abusive marriages. A lack of respect for one's spouse shuts down meaningful communication and results in unresolved conflict, a lack of trust, and resentment. Blame doesn't want to resolve conflicts constructively. Blame wants to be *right*.

And speaking of being "right," I offer a word of caution about blaming your spouse to others (such as your friends, your children's teachers, fellow PTA members, or your attorney). Speaking negatively to others about how awful your spouse was (or is) will only backfire on you. Understand that whomever you're speaking with is more likely to attribute the negativity to you rather than to your spouse. This concept is known as spontaneous trait transference.

I listen for blame in every meeting with a new, prospective divorce client. What I now know is that someone with a persistent blame story is going to be a difficult person to represent, and I usually decline the representation. Why? A persistent blame story, especially one that casts the other spouse as completely flawed and responsible for the marriage's collapse, gets in the way of resolving the case. Not only is the blamer unwilling to take some responsibility for the demise of the marriage, but the blamer also generally refuses to take much responsibility for helping resolve the issues in the legal divorce. Instead, it's common for the blamer to adopt unreasonable positions, which actually forestall the resolution of the divorce. The feeling I get is that they want to make the other spouse pay dearly during the process.

This is because blame rests on a huge undercurrent of unresolved anger and conflict, as mentioned earlier. When that anger cannot be vindicated within the context of the legal process (which often doesn't occur), their anger seeks an outlet elsewhere. When the blamer isn't vindicated by the court, the anger is often transferred from the opposing spouse on to the blamer's attorney. The result is that the attorney stands in the place of the opposing spouse and is blamed unconsciously for the all the wrongs in the marriage, and consciously for any perceived flaws in the divorce settlement or outcome.

But someone has to be responsible for the ending of a marriage, right? My response is: of course. Both partners are responsible for the demise of their marriage (even if one partner is only 2 percent responsible!), which is why divorce is such a prime opportunity for self-reflection and personal growth.

And herein lies the way out of blaming! What if, instead of saying "It's my fault," or projecting the responsibility onto our ex-spouses, we could believe that the divorce brought with it lessons for everyone involved? What if we retooled responsibility as a way to learn and grow from our own mistakes, and those of our partners?

We don't need to be the judge and the jury. What we need to do is separate the deed from the doer and the sin from the sinner, because at our core, we're all the beloveds of the Beloved. It is also helpful to remember that the definition of the word "sin" comes from the Greek word for sin: *hamartia*. The word was historically used in the context of archery, and this phrase literally means "to miss the mark." It definitely doesn't translate into a mantra that someone is wrong, wrong, wrong, forever and ever and ever. No.

Reclaiming our fair share of personal responsibility also facilitates two very important things which aid both in resolving the divorce and living life manageably in its aftermath.

First, being personally responsible enables problem solving. Einstein said that we cannot solve a problem from the level of thinking that created it. If we initially believed that the "problem" was someone else's to begin with, we can help resolve it simply by admitting that we may have played some part in helping create it.

Huh?

Well, this works because, when we take ownership over some portion of the problem, it's natural for us to also take some amount of responsibility for helping fix the issue, allowing all sorts of new options and possibilities to surface for repairing the problem.

Second, if you have minor children with your spouse, you are probably going to have to coparent with this person after the divorce is concluded. Do you want this postdivorce parenting relationship to be characterized by unresolved conflict, a lack of trust, and resentment? Do you think this would be good for your kids? I hope your answer to these questions is "no," both for your own well-being and that of your children. Learning to focus on solutions (as opposed to judgments), admitting mistakes when they occur, and apologizing go a long way in creating a functional coparenting relationship. In fact, the research shows that being able to apologize in any relationship makes it much more likely to thrive.

While our marriages may not have thrived, we can learn from them. It was Maya Angelou who said, "Then when you know better, do better." We can use our mistakes, and those of our spouses, as catalysts for personal growth and transformation. This will only work, though, if we can get past our own blame stories.

Keeping Your Emotional Balance during the Process of Divorce

One of the biggest ways you can maintain your emotional balance during the divorce is to choose to respond—instead of react—to situations around you.

What's the difference?

For our purposes, a *reaction* is basically an emotional retort, fired off almost immediately on the heels of receiving some disturbing news (from your spouse, your kids, your attorney, the court, and so forth). In contrast, a *response* is a thoughtful reply. It usually results from taking time to reflect on the situation or issue, and answering from a place that corresponds to your highest values.

Why bother taking the time to respond instead of react? Why not unload (on your spouse, especially!) with both barrels? Why be calm?

By no means am I suggesting that you "stuff your feelings." If you feel angry at something your spouse, your attorney, or the court did, then, by all means, feel the anger. What I'm suggesting here is that you may want to think twice about issuing your reply from this place. And here's why.

To begin with, reactivity tends to feed reactivity. You react, and then your spouse reacts, and now there's a chain reaction that has been set in motion. I suspect you likely experienced something like this when you were married. Remember those fights where, by the end of them, you couldn't even remember what topic had started them? Yeah. Same thing here; only during the divorce, you might be paying two attorneys $250 per hour *each* to deal with your chain reaction.

Also, consider that reacting comes from a place of being physiologically fired up because of our intense emotions. A retort from this place is from a place of anger and will often leave you with a bad case of buyer's remorse, wishing you hadn't communicated from this frame of mind.

Remember that when you feel emotionally triggered, your fight or flight system is activated. As we've talked about, this response serves us well when we need to swerve to avoid a deer in the road or react quickly to keep a toddler from injuring herself. But as you have likely already experienced in your own life, this physiological response does not serve you quite as well when your spouse texts you that he is going to be forty-five minutes late with the kids on Sunday evening (at the conclusion of his weekend of parenting time), and that the kids' homework isn't done.

Sure, you could explode at him in a reactive text, and then he could fire several reactive texts back at you—all while driving the children in the car. Or you could call him, and proceed to engage in a venomous argument with the children present in the background and witness to the whole debacle.

Or you could take a deep breath and buy yourself some time before replying to your spouse. Write out on a piece of paper the nasty text you would like to send, and then rip the paper into little shreds or burn it. Discharging the anger will help you think more clearly. Set a timer. Go for a walk. Call a friend. Do whatever you need to do to distance yourself from the initial reaction you're having. You will need to keep yourself occupied for at least thirty minutes, which is how long it takes for your physiology to calm down after the triggering event.

Once you are calmed down, I suggest you decide to respond from a place that honors your highest values. In the last example, if your children's well-being is one of your highest values, then your response will need to take their needs into consideration. "Love your kids more than you hate your spouse," as the saying goes. If you know that your spouse will likely react to your text or call in front of your children, then don't send the text or make the call when your kids are with your spouse. No child wants to witness his parents fighting or hear one parent talk poorly of the other. In addition, you would want to keep your children calm in this example, because when they get home, they are going to need to complete their homework. If honesty is one of your top values, you can preserve the issue of your spouse's tardy drop-off for future discussion with your spouse by simply responding,

"We'll have to discuss this tomorrow. I need to focus on helping the kids get their homework done tonight."

Responding also works really well when it comes time to exchange and consider settlement proposals. It can be very easy to react to a portion of your spouse's proposal that offends you, and then completely shut down about the other issues. The problem with this is that the way in which your spouse is proposing to resolve some (or all) of the other issues may be acceptable to you. Don't throw out the proverbial baby with the bath water. If you can respond instead of react, you can hold on to the baby (your needs), and negotiate for some fresh, warm bath water!

Controlling the Controllable

One of the hardest things for all divorcing people to realize and accept is that they are not in total control of either the process or the resolution of the divorce. Actually, many players are involved in getting through and finalizing the divorce, including: your spouse, your attorney, your spouse's attorney, the judicial officer assigned to your case, the mediator with whom you're working, your spouse's new paramour, your new paramour, your spouse's family, your family—the list goes on and on.

Along with the many players at work in the divorce, there are also differing perspectives about the "right" outcome of a divorce. What may seem like a totally reasonable alimony proposal to you may be laughable to your spouse—and there could even be case law in your state to support both positions! Sometimes, despite your very best efforts and those of your attorney, you do not get the outcome you desire. This is disheartening for my clients. I have had this happen, for example, with male and female breadwinners alike, who are required to pay spousal maintenance to a philandering, unemployed spouse—in addition to equitably sharing the marital assets.

So, how do you get comfortable with the unknowns (how long, how much, uncertain outcomes) in your divorce? The only way to find any comfort in the discomfort is to realize what items you do control, and to make the best decisions about those items with the information available to you. And you have to find a way to be at peace with the uncertain resolution of the other items. You may handle this is any number of ways, which include surrendering to a higher power, working with a therapist, and other positive solutions.

Regardless, one item you can *always* choose to control is *your* response. Some of the breadwinners I described in the previous paragraph, while disappointed in the spousal maintenance award to their spouse, were able to brush off the result quickly; others stewed. The ones who readily came to terms with the outcome were able to see something good about the decision that gave them a measure of peace. One client said to me, "Well, it will just go toward making a nice home for my kids, anyway."

Fighting as the Last Form of Intimacy

Naturally, the level of intimacy between a divorcing couple varies greatly. Some couples can maintain a comfortable, platonic connection for the benefit of their kids, while others cannot stand the sight of their ex-spouses. For many couples, the intimacy between them eventually dies and is ultimately replaced with acceptance, sadness, or wherever the individuals settle in with respect to the stages of grief.

During the grieving process, however, and especially close to the finality of the legal divorce, something interesting happens on a predictable basis. As the legal divorce nears its conclusion, you think that the couple would be happy and would rush to finish the process. It is usually just the opposite. What I see more often than not is what looks like one or both spouses not wanting to be done. Fighting ensues, and the saga continues with a final stand-off that has to be resolved before the divorce can be finalized.

This scenario is so predictable that I spoke to a friend of mine, who is both therapist and divorce coach, about it. Her response was that in the shadow of finality, many people feel scared. They don't want things to be done and over with, and aren't ready to begin anew. So what do they do? They unconsciously stretch out the conflict to avoid the psychological discomfort of the finality of the divorce.

If this happens in your case, first of all, just know that this is very common. In my caseload, I estimate this happens approximately 75 percent of the time. Often, the conflict is short-lived. There are occasions, though, when the conflict drags on simply because one spouse's "divorce readiness" is still too low for them to agree to conclude the divorce.

If you are not quite ready to be divorced and are creating conflict in your case, take time to work through your feelings, ideally with some professional help to guide you. If your spouse is creating conflict to extend the divorce, then also take your time. It is best to do the opposite of what you likely want to do. Pushing your spouse to finalize the divorce will only serve to make him or her more reactive. Instead, a better option is to give your spouse space to process these emotions. If the matter drags on too long, judicial intervention is always available to bring finality to the process, although it's rarely necessary. Most of these "final stands" lose their bluster within a couple of weeks, as the objecting spouse works through the emotions and realizes that delaying the matter only costs time and money, which are both generally in short supply during divorce.

Domestic Abuse

Abuse between spouses is an unfortunate reality in many divorces. In fact, the American Bar Association estimates that 1.3 million women and 835,000 men are physically assaulted by an intimate partner each year.[9]

What is domestic abuse? The answer is that it is usually defined by state statute. In the state in which I am licensed to practice, domestic abuse is defined as actual physical harm, or fear of the imminent infliction of physical harm, or terroristic threats, between family or household members.

It may surprise you to learn that mental or emotional abuse, or financial control and manipulation, may not be included in the statutory definition of domestic abuse. Just because these types of abuse are absent from the statutory definition of domestic abuse doesn't mean they don't exist! They do exist, and in some ways, they are even more damaging to a person's psyche than physical abuse. Further, these types of abuse can be brought up in the divorce, but they may or may not qualify as "domestic abuse" as defined by your state's civil or criminal statutes.

That said, it is important for you to know that your state may have both civil and criminal repercussions for domestic abuse. For example, if you have experienced domestic abuse, your partner may be indicted for domestic assault (a criminal charge), and you may qualify for an order for protection or restraining order (these are usually civil remedies). So, if your case involves domestic abuse, it is important to research what criminal and civil options are available in your state for redressing this situation.

An admission, or finding (by a court of law), of domestic abuse may affect certain issues in your divorce case, including custody (legal and physical), as well as parenting time. In the state in which I practice, as well as other jurisdictions, an admission or finding of domestic abuse creates a presumption against the sharing of custody (meaning that joint legal and/or joint physical custody may not be appropriate). Why? Because joint custody requires a lot of interaction and cooperation between the parties, which may not be possible in relationships in which domestic abuse has occurred.

Further, if domestic abuse is present in your case, you may want to think twice about participating in mediation (the process of dispute resolution where the parties try and work things out with the help of a third party—the mediator). Why? Many experts in the field of domestic abuse believe that mediation, especially if attended without attorneys, can create a prime opportunity for continued abuse, manipulation, and control between the parties. In addition, any resulting "agreements" from mediation may have occurred, or been influenced by, the continuation of abuse in that context. In other words, the abuser may be able to abuse, control, or manipulate the abused party, such that the abused party gives up and agrees to an unfair settlement just to end the abuse, control, or manipulation.

If you feel that domestic abuse may be present (or was present at some point) in your marriage, then you need to be aware that there is a predictable cycle of domestic abuse and that you have resources to help you understand, and get out of it. (I have included the cycle of domestic abuse in appendix E for your reference.) Further, you may have local or state resources available to help you. There are also national organizations that may be able to provide education and assistance. Some of these national organizations include: National Domestic Violence Hotline (800-799-7233); Rape, Abuse and Incest National Network (RAINN) (800-656-HOPE); Family Violence Prevention Fund (800-595-4889); and National Coalition Against Domestic Violence (303-839-1852).

Whether you're the initiating spouse or the responding spouse, the emotional layering of a divorce is considerably more textured than the legal component. To ease your way through the challenging terrain of the emotional roller coaster of divorce, let's recap some strategies you can adopt that will help you find your way.

1. Cultivate a gratitude practice. Research indicates even a short few minutes of conscious gratitude alleviates stress and has a lasting positive effect.

2. Make a short, three-item list—one time—of attributes of your ex about which you are grateful. Keep this short list top of mind so that when you're torqued, you can focus on the good.

3. Make a conscious effort to respond instead of react to your spouse. Even if your spouse goes above and beyond to make things difficult for you, choosing a response instead of a reaction will make a far more positive impact on the overall resolution of your divorce, especially if you have kids.

Take care of yourself during this time and get the support you need. Again, whether you need to work with a therapist to unpack deep-seated emotional issues or would prefer to hire a divorce coach to guide you through the emotional divorce, make sure you get the support you need during this challenging time. It will make all the difference.

The Financial Divorce

Well, we've made it through the legal and emotional aspects of divorce, and now we're on to the financial. In this chapter, we'll talk about what you need to know about your finances, and we'll start with what you need to know as you begin the divorce (and start to acquire information about the process). We'll also discuss what happens as you start to negotiate the financial issues in the divorce, and we will discuss how not all assets are created equal. Then, we'll progress into what you may want to consider doing with the assets that you're awarded from the marriage after you're divorced.

But first, let's tackle a big issue I see all the time, mostly in women, but in some men, too. Some folks are just plain scared to death about having to tackle the financial issues, because they've not been the partner in the marriage who has paid the bills, balanced the checkbook, or made the investment decisions.

I'm Scared! I'm Not Familiar with Our Finances!

First, breathe! It's okay—you're not alone! A lot of couples divide up marital responsibilities, including who manages the finances (such as bill paying or investment decisions). And you can get up-to-speed quickly on what you need to know to be informed about your finances as you go through the divorce.

Often, what bubbles up, from underneath the lack of familiarity with the finances, is a much, much deeper fear of being penniless and homeless. In women, I refer to something I mentioned earlier called the *bag lady syndrome*. With men, I hear it described as a fear of "living in a cardboard box under the bridge." Regardless of how much money they may have (some have millions of dollars), many men and women worry greatly that they will end up with no financial resources as a result of the divorce.

What will help ease this deep-seated fear is *knowledge*, both as to the state of your current finances, but also with respect to cultivating a basic understanding of financial management. We'll talk about these issues in just a few paragraphs.

Therapy will also help you manage, and perhaps overcome, these fears. Why therapy? What seems to drive the "bag lady/living under the bridge" syndromes is often basic lack of both worthiness (in one's self) and trust (in life), as well as a negative perception that the world works against, rather than for, people. This manifests in thoughts like: "People never watch out for me; I always seem to get the short end of the stick in life" and so forth. These aren't issues that the legal system can redress, other than to reassure you that you are, indeed, entitled to either an equal or an equitable share of the marital resources. That's why therapy is essential if you may have these deep-seated fears.

Knowledge (and Compiling Information!) Is Power

Whether you know nothing about your family's finances or assets, or everything, the first step in getting prepared for the financial aspect of divorce is to compile and copy all the information you have access to regarding your finances. Also, ask your attorney if you should make a second copy for your spouse (or your spouse's attorney), which may save your attorney from having to do so (and this will save you money!).

The reason for compiling and copying this information is so that you (and your attorney) have a broad understanding as to the overall marital financial landscape. Specifically, you will need to collect and copy information as it relates to your family's income, monthly expenses, assets, and liabilities. Let's take this step-by-step.

INCOME

First, you'll need to know everything about your and your spouse's respective incomes. Make copies of your federal and state income tax returns, along with all of the attachments (W-2s, 1099s, and so forth) for the last three to five years. If you have an accountant, you can usually get copies from them. Make copies of the last year's worth of paycheck stubs for both you and your spouse. Also, to begin with, get copies of your current bank statements, although you may need bank statements for the last several months or year.

MONTHLY EXPENSES

In addition to your income information, you will need to document your current monthly expenses. Most divorce attorneys use a form (like the one I've provided in appendix F). You will need to fill this out and make copies of your current bills. Many people now use a bill pay service, and that's a great way to document the extent of your monthly expenses. Otherwise, make a copy of your check book register and bank statements, as well as copies of the bills you pay on a monthly basis. The documentation of monthly expenses is important and helps to extinguish the argument that your monthly expenses may be either unknown or inflated.

ASSETS

Your attorney will also need copies of documents that substantiate the assets you and your spouse have acquired during the marriage. (We discussed this in chapter 5.) To recap, you'll need your current tax statements for the homestead (and any other parcels of real property you may own), recent statements for all retirement plans and investment accounts, current statements for all bank accounts (checking, savings, 529s, and CDs,), values for your vehicles (see kbb.com or nada.com). Basically, anything that you own which has a value of $500 or more, generally has to be documented and valued.

LIABILITIES

You will also need to make copies of your current liabilities. This means get copies of your mortgage statement(s). Make copies of your monthly installment payments for your car, motorcycle, boat, and the like. Get up-to-date copies of all credit card statements. Locate and copy any student loan statements as well as any personal loans that you may have with friends or family members. If you've paid a retainer to your attorney, you should also get some sort of statement (credit card or billing invoice) for this, too.

Make Timely Payments and Keep Bills Current

I used to do divorce presentations years ago with a financial planner. When asked what she thought was the most important thing to remember about finances during the divorce, her response was always the same: preserve your FICO score by making timely payments on your outstanding financial obligations.

What is a FICO score anyway? Your FICO score is your credit rating, as determined by a company now called FICO (formerly Fair Isaac Co.). They figure out your credit rating by pulling and analyzing your credit information from the three big credit reporting agencies in the US, including Experian, Equifax, and TransUnion. Once determined, your FICO score is the number one way in which a lender will evaluate your request for credit.

You want to keep your bills current, and your FICO score high, throughout the divorce. This is because you may well have a need for credit during, or after, the divorce. For example, you may want to purchase a homestead. Or you may want to open a new credit card in your name only with a sizable credit limit as a buffer to pay for unforeseen expenses or attorney's fees. But you likely won't be able to do either if you have a low FICO score as a result of several late payments on your outstanding debts.

I will also say that making timely payments on your outstanding obligations is smart for another reason. Divorce is a stressful event in and of itself. The stress of the divorce can be compounded exponentially by having to deal with collection calls, foreclosure notices, or a simultaneous bankruptcy proceeding.

What if you simply can't pay all your bills during the divorce? If possible, I would look to family members or friends for help, if they're able and willing. If that's not an option, then some states have assistance programs for certain expenses, like gas and electricity, which may be of benefit. Otherwise, it can be very difficult, because invariably in divorce, expenses increase (and often double) at the same time the family's combined income is split between the divorcing couple. So, if you have credit blight during divorce, take heart. You're not alone. The best thing you can do is get through the divorce, and rebuild your credit step-by-step afterward.

What to Do with Joint Bank Accounts and Joint Credit Cards

Let's say you have a joint savings account with your spouse, into which both of your paychecks are deposited every two weeks. You and your spouse also have a joint checking account at the same financial institution. It's used to pay several of your joint expenses, with money that is transferred from the joint savings account. In addition, you two have a joint credit card, on which you charge miscellaneous monthly expenses to take advantage of miles or bonus points.

And let's also say you were just served with divorce papers. The divorce has commenced. Now what with respect to these joint accounts?

First, remember how important it is to preserve your FICO score during the divorce. So, at least for the time being, the status quo should be maintained. Paychecks should still go into the joint savings account, and bills should continue to be paid on a timely basis from the joint checking account. And you should also stay current with respect to the payments on the joint credit card. You can consider capping the amount of credit available on the card, in the event your spouse starts to become a spendthrift; but otherwise, I would recommend leaving the credit card alone.

Admittedly, this isn't the way things play out sometimes. You may get served, and then find out that your spouse has withdrawn all of the money from the savings account (including your paycheck!), and there's nothing left to cover either the credit card bill or the bills paid from the joint checking account. What then?

The first thing to do is to call your spouse on this duplicitous behavior. Ask them to return to the money to either the joint savings or checking account to cover the bills that need to be paid. If this doesn't work, then you need to interview and retain an attorney sooner than later. The attorney then needs to approach your spouse (if they're not represented), or the opposing attorney, or the court to seek redress. Not only should your attorney try to get the money returned, but there has to be a plan for how the bills are going to be paid on a go-forward basis. You also need to open an individual checking account, into which you can reroute your paychecks, in the event that your spouse refuses to return the money and continues to use the joint savings and checking accounts.

If your spouse no longer wants to use the joint savings and checking accounts, then they'll eventually need to be closed, but only after the bills that are paid from the checking account are rerouted to someone's individual account. So, for example, if it is decided that your spouse is going to stay in the homestead during the divorce, then they're often expected to pay the bills that are related to living in the homestead (think: mortgage, utilities, and cable). If your car payment was formerly taken out of the joint account, then it's probably rerouted to your individual checking account, as long as you have the income to pay it. Same goes for your spouse's vehicle payment. Don't forget to work out who's going to pay the bills that may be paid less frequently, such as the water bill or the car insurance.

Eventually, though, the joint checking and savings accounts will be closed. For some couples, this comes after they're divorced, as they use the accounts throughout the divorce. For others, it happens at the outset of the divorce. Ideally, the joint credit card will eventually be closed as well. I suggest that you open a credit card account in your name only (if you don't already have one). If the joint credit card has a balance, this balance will need to be rolled onto individual credit cards (based on your agreement as to how to pay the joint credit card balance) as a part of the divorce. You do not want to have a spouse simply assume the payments for the joint credit card, if this can be avoided, because if timely payments are not made, your credit will be blemished.

Not All Assets Are Created Equal!

As you proceed through your divorce, you will need to decide which assets you would prefer to have and which ones you are willing to let go, since you can't generally have them all! In thinking about this, there is some information about which you should be aware.

First, it is not unusual for the both people, generally, and women specifically, to want to keep the homestead after the divorce. When there are minor children involved, there seems to be a desire to keep them in the same residence to maintain stability and continuity.

Even so, it is not always possible—or advisable—to keep the house. Finances are almost always tight, and the homestead may no longer be affordable. Further, the house is not usually the best investment, from the perspective of future appreciation.

Historically speaking, investments (including investment accounts and retirement assets) tend to appreciate at a far greater rate than residential real estate. When calculated over a longer period of time, residential real estate appreciates on an average of about 3 percent per year. Investments almost always do better, and over the last seventy years, they have appreciated at approximately 8 percent per year. This means that investments tend to do almost three times better than residential real estate in the long run.

In short, whoever elects to keep the homestead—and it is often the woman—tends to end up with an asset that may likely be worth far less over time. In my experience, the time-value of investments and retirement assets can be hard to make up. That is to say, if you lose assets that you and your spouse have invested in, and which have appreciated over time (say a twenty-year marriage), it can be difficult to find the money to invest to replenish these accounts and recoup the appreciation and compounding that occurred over those twenty years. To make up these monies, which I am assuming were traded for the equity in the homestead, you'll have to save at a much higher rate going forward to make up for this loss. And since budgets are stretched to the limits in almost every divorce, increasing the rate of savings for retirement can be nearly impossible. The result is that the loss of retirement investments is rarely—if ever—made up, and that leaves the spouse who opted for keeping the homestead ill-prepared when it comes time to transition to retirement. So, this is not to be taken lightly.

In addition, you need to be aware that some assets have future tax consequences associated with them. Monies invested in tax-deferred retirement plans, for example, will have taxes that need to be paid in the future, when the money is eventually withdrawn. If the withdrawal is imminent, or if we can pretty clearly estimate the future tax liability, then it's not unusual to reduce value of the retirement or investment asset by the amount of the taxes that will be due and owing. Otherwise, if you take a $25,000 retirement account (that has a future tax consequence associated with it) and your spouse gets $25,000 in cash, you are actually getting an asset of lesser value, due to the taxes you will one day have to pay when you withdraw the retirement monies.

For this reason, it is not unusual for parties to divide cash accounts and retirement plans equally, as opposed to exchanging cash assets (or other assets with no tax implications) for "tax-pregnant" assets. For example, if you have $20,000 in a Roth IRA (taxes have already been paid on the asset), and $20,000 in a traditional IRA (taxes will have to be paid on this asset at the time of withdrawal), I would suggest the equal division of both IRAs, as opposed to awarding one of you the traditional IRA and the other the Roth IRA. The Roth IRA is clearly the more valuable asset, as there will be no taxes due when these monies are eventually withdrawn. When the monies in the traditional IRA are eventually withdrawn, they will be reduced by your income tax rates at the time of the withdrawal. What happens if your combined state and federal income tax rate is then 22 percent? Then your asset would be worth 22 percent less than the Roth IRA, right off the top!

You also need to be aware of whether there may be capital gains taxes looming in your various assets. If you are taking a parcel of real property (such as the homestead or a rental property) that has appreciated, then you want to clearly understand whether there may be a capital gains issue when it comes time to sell the property.

Often, I see the issue of capital gains lurking about in stock owned by the former couple. Say you and your spouse own stock in ten different companies. You're going to need to find out when you purchased the shares (and at what price), in addition to what the shares are now worth. If you've sold any shares in the interim, you will probably need to know this information as well. (It can usually be found on your income tax returns.)

Why do we care about the purchase price and the current value of stock? Well, let's say you and your spouse bought 100 shares of Google at $85 per share at its initial public offering in August 2004. Fast forward to 2015. You're now getting a divorce. You and your spouse still own the 100 shares you purchased in 2004, but now they're worth $544 per share. Guess what? There is an impending capital gains tax burden on these shares. In other words, this asset is "tax-pregnant."

You bought the shares for $8,500 (100 shares x $85/share), but now they're worth $54,400 (100 shares x $544/share)! Good for you! And, of course, the government wants its share in the boon attributable to your investing acumen (or just plain good luck!) in the form of capital gains taxes. So, let's assume you'll pay 15 percent in capital gains taxes to the federal government, plus your state capital gains rate (say 7 percent). So, there is a $10,098 tax bill ($54,400 - $8,500 = $45,900; $45,900 x .22 = $10,098) that is looming for this asset alone!

Given this, you and your spouse may want to liquidate this asset, and pay the taxes (perhaps as a married couple through a joint tax return). Or, you may want to take the Google stock, but only at a price that is net of the taxes that would be due and owing now. That is to say, you would want to take the asset for $44,302 ($54,400 less estimated taxes of $10,098) and not $54,400. Maybe you and your spouse just want to divide up the Google shares between you. Whatever works for you and your spouse is great, as long as the decision is an *informed* one, in light of the taxes that will have to be paid on this asset.

As you can see, not all assets are created equal. You have to be aware of the tax implications associated with each of your assets. These conversations should occur between you, your attorney, and your accountant, if you have one. If you are not represented by an attorney or an accountant, then you have some research to do. Otherwise, you could end up being awarded assets that do not have the same value as those awarded to your spouse.

Basic Financial Management

While I am not a financial planner, I work with them in my divorce cases all the time. I also have a financial planner, who has given me a lot of excellent guidance when it comes to financial management. So, I can give you some very basic information about financial management, though I strongly suggest that you seek out and meet with a financial planner to learn more about these important concepts.

Every financial planner I know starts out by determining what your monthly expenses currently are, or perhaps, what they're going to be on a go-forward basis. You'll have to determine this as a part of your divorce so you'll have this base covered.

In looking at your monthly expenses, the financial planner will often be concerned with your rate of savings—and not just for retirement. Ideally, financial planners like to see their clients have an emergency savings account, in addition to a general savings account for things like travel, new car purchases, and so forth.

The financial planner then takes a look at your income. This may come from earnings, child support, spousal maintenance, interest, dividends, rents paid to you, or perhaps you receive gifted monies on a regular basis.

If your income currently meets or exceeds all of your expenses, great! Then the issue becomes planning for changes to your income and expenses *over time*. What does this mean? Well, like when your kids head off to college, or when you'd like to retire. We'll talk about visioning and planning for new financial dreams and goals in just a minute.

But what if your income doesn't cover all your present expenses? Unfortunately, this is the reality for a lot of people. And there are only three answers to this predicament: 1) increase your income, 2) decrease your expenses, or 3) both. No financial planner will suggest deficit financing as a means to consistently meet your monthly expenses.

There are also some general rules of thumb to know about when you consider buying a home or how much to save for retirement. Most mortgage lenders say that your monthly PITI (principal, interest, taxes, and insurance) should not be over 28 percent of your gross monthly income. So, for example, if your gross monthly income is

$5,000 per month ($60,000 per year), then your monthly PITI should be no more than $1,400 per month ($16,800 per year).

With regard to retirement savings, Fidelity estimates that you'll need eight times your final salary when you retire. The idea here is to not outlive your retirement savings over twenty-five years of anticipated retirement (that is from age sixty-five to ninety). Fidelity estimates that you should have one times your retirement saved by age thirty-five; three times saved by age forty-five; and five times by age fifty-five.

Today Isn't Tomorrow: Cultivating and Planning For New Financial Dreams

After your divorce, you are going to have reenvision your life, including your financial goals and dreams. You are also going to have to remember that today isn't tomorrow. Why? Because finances can be really tight right after the divorce is concluded, and you may find yourself living month-to-month. This isn't necessarily how things will always be, and it's important to have a vision for your financial future to help guide your spending decisions now.

Some financial goals will have to be restructured. If you have a seventeen-year-old son who is going to attend college next year, and you want to help him with tuition, room, and board, then you may have to forestall your retirement to do so. Maybe you would like to buy a house like the marital homestead, but cannot currently afford the down payment.

In these examples, the question is one of priorities. If your priority is to assist your son with college, then that may take precedent over retiring at age sixty-five. If you want to save for a down payment for a homestead similar to the marital homestead, then you may choose to forego vacations or eating out frequently, for example, to be able to accumulate the down payment sooner than later.

Whatever your priorities are, it's good to know them! You can't shoot an arrow if you don't have a target. Similarly, you can't plan for your future if you haven't envisioned an end game.

The overview of this whole chapter starts and ends with picking your head up, taking a deep breath, and looking soberly at your finances. Knowledge and clarity really do bring a sense of peace. Here is a list for you to track your financials as you wade through this component of preparing for divorce.

Make copies of all the financial documents to which you have access, including:

1. **INCOME**
   - Your paycheck stubs from January 1 to present
   - Spouse's paycheck stubs from January 1 to present
   - Tax returns (state and federal) for the last three years
   - US Social Security records reflecting earnings and qualifications for retirement benefits. (Online at: ssa.gov or contact Social Security at 1-800-772-1213)
   - Other (all documents that could be used to establish your or spouse's income)

2. **REAL ESTATE (FOR EVERYTHING OWNED BY YOU OR YOUR SPOUSE)**
   - Warranty deed or quit claim deed (deed showing legal description not just county tax statement)
   - County tax statement (current)
   - Mortgage statement or contact for deed statement (current)
   - Purchase agreement, settlement statement, other documentation regarding purchase

3. **ASSETS (FOR EVERYTHING OWNED BY YOU OR YOUR SPOUSE)**

   - Cash accounts such as savings, checking, and money market (current statements for each account)

   - Business and professional interests
     - Business tax returns (last three years)
     - Profit/loss and balance sheet (current)
     - All other relevant documentation

   - Savings passbooks and savings certificates

   - Corporate stocks and stock certificates

   - Insurance policies (life/disability/long-term care); information on the owner, insured, beneficiary, cash value, and annual premium

   - Group benefit and insurance information from your employer/spouse's employer
     - Life insurance summary of benefits
     - Disability insurance summary of benefits
     - Medical insurance summary (cost of employee only, cost to add children, cost for family)

   - Retirement plan documents (statements)
     - IRA, 401(k), 403(b), etc.
     - Pension plan statements (Provide a statement showing the monthly benefit assuming you terminate employment today. This can usually be obtained online, from HR, or from the pension administrator.)

   - Investment accounts, stocks, stock options, and profit sharing (current statements reflecting interest and value)

- Motor vehicles
    - Print off "private party value" for each vehicle on Kelly Blue Book (kbb.com)
    - RVs, snowmobiles, boats, classic cars—print off "book" value for each vehicle on NADA (nada.com)
- Other (financial statements for the last five years prepared by you or spouse for securing loans or for any other purpose)

4. **LIABILITIES (FOR EVERYTHING OWNED BY YOU OR YOUR SPOUSE)**

    - Statements for all secured or unsecured debt amounts (credit cards, medical bills, personal loans, etc.)

5. **LEGAL DOCUMENTS (FOR YOU OR YOUR SPOUSE)**

    - All legal documents relating to this proceeding or prior divorce

At this point you may also wish to list your financial goals for two and five years postdivorce.

Having this information isn't the be-all and end-all to quell your anxiety, but knowing where you stand will certainly make this part of the process far less intimidating.

It's Over! Now What?

Your attorney calls you. She just received notice that your final divorce paperwork, known as your *judgment and decree*, has been entered by the court . . . and you are officially divorced.

How are you feeling? Some clients express happiness at this news; others feel sad and disappointed. Many clients thank me for the call, and then take their leave of me to process this information. Regardless, most of my clients seem to think that the divorce is now over.

But hold on! What is all done, and legally severed, are the bonds of matrimony. The parenting time schedule is in place. The support obligations have been set. The assets and liabilities have been divided. Despite these hallmarks of finality, there are still legal and emotional issues that need to be resolved before my clients are completely through with their divorces.

Legal Clean-Up

After the judgment and decree is entered, there is often legal work that needs to be completed to preserve the finality of the divorce and to protect your now-separate interests.

NOTICE OF FILING ORDER

First, we usually have to serve (on the opposing attorney or ex-spouse) and file (with the court) what's called a *notice of filing order*. This notice basically says to the other side: "Hey, the divorce is final, and if, for some reason, you don't like it, you only have this many days to appeal the judgment and decree." Because most cases settle, the notice of filing order is just part of the final stages of legal paperwork. That is to say, your spouse is unlikely to appeal the terms of the already agreed-upon judgment and decree.

If, however, your case went to trial to resolve some (or all) of the issues of your divorce, and you received the trial court's decision (and liked it), you would want to serve and file the notice of filing order right away. Why? Because you want to start the clock ticking with respect to your ex-spouse's time to appeal.

POSTTRIAL MOTIONS AND APPEALS

In most jurisdictions, the time frame to file an appeal is limited from anywhere between sixty and ninety days after the receipt of the notice of filing order. Will your case be appealed? Probably not. Most cases (approximately 95 percent) are settled by an agreement between the parties, and are almost never appealed. Of the 5 percent of cases resolved by trial, I would estimate that fewer than 5 percent end up being appealed. So, statistically speaking, it is pretty unlikely that your case will be appealed.

If your case was resolved by a trial, it is possible that either party could bring posttrial motions, in which they would essentially ask the judge to change the outcome of the case. Sometimes posttrial motions are the precursors to an appeal, and sometimes they are not.

If your case does end up being appealed, only a limited number of issues are usually presented to the appellate court—not the whole case. For example, maybe your spouse is really unhappy with two issues, namely, being ordered to pay you maintenance and contribute to your attorney's fees. These are the issues that would likely be appealed—not custody, parenting time, child support, or property allocation.

During the appeal, all of the terms of your judgment and decree remain in full force and effect. Support (child, spousal) is due and owing, the parenting time schedule is followed, and all uncontested assets and liabilities are divided up.

The appeal itself is a process with a beginning, a middle, and an end. It usually begins with the service and filing of a *notice of appeal*. Once this notice is filed, many jurisdictions now require the divorcing couple (and their attorneys) to participate in mediation to try and resolve the issue(s). If mediation is successful, then the resolution is incorporated into the parties' final legal paperwork, and that's it. If mediation is unsuccessful, then the now-divorced couple (or their attorneys) will have to prepare, serve, and file appellate briefs (which are formal written documents) in strict accordance with the rules for the appellate court procedure in that state.

Most appealed court cases are argued orally before the appellate court, but only after each individual's formal documents have been served and filed. While oral arguments can sometimes be waived, most people who push for an appeal want to have their "day in court." After the oral argument, the appellate court record is usually closed, and the court will then take the matter under consideration. The final written decision isn't issued until later—often several months after the oral argument.

The appellate court may decide to uphold the lower court's ruling or reverse it (in whole or in part). The appellate court could also remand (meaning return) the case to the lower court for further proceedings, if necessary.

REAL PROPERTY

While appeals are rare (thankfully!), most cases still do have some amount of legal clean-up work that needs to be done once the judgment and decree has been entered. For example, if you were awarded real property as a part of the divorce, then title to this property has to be changed to reflect that you now own it by yourself. This process is pretty straightforward and involves the use of what is known as a *quit claim deed*. A quit claim deed is a very short (usually one page) legal document that transfers your ex-spouse's interest in the real property to you. The document is signed by your ex-spouse, and then filed with the county recorder (or registrar) to legally establish that you are now the sole owner of the property, or vice versa if that's the case.

In some jurisdictions, you can also use what's known as a summary real estate disposition judgment (SREDJ) to transfer the interest in property from one person to the other. In fact, I prefer the use of the SREDJ, because it doesn't require the signature of the other person (unlike the quit claim deed). We can draft the document and send it for review and signature to the same judge who signed off on the judgment and decree. Once the judge has signed off on the SREDJ and filed it with the court administrator, we order a certified copy of the document and file it with the county recorder (or registrar). In my opinion, the whole process with a SREDJ is more streamlined, and there is no room for "gamesmanship" by the ex-spouse, such as delaying the signing and returning of the quit claim deed as a means to get back at my client.

In addition to transferring the title(s) to the real property, often my clients also have to refinance the mortgage(s) linked to the real property awarded to them. Refinancing is often required, because the other person—naturally—does not want to continue to be liable under the original terms of the mortgage and promissory note obtained in the names of both parties. (Note: the mortgage turns the real property into collateral to secure the payment of the debt related it. The promissory note, which is almost always required in addition to a mortgage, is different in that it makes each owner personally liable to repay the debt incurred to purchase the property.) Unless refinancing occurs, both people remain liable under the existing mortgage and promissory note. So, if late payments are made, each person's credit score is affected—even though the judgment and decree may require only one of them to service the debt. Each party's relationship to the mortgagee (the company that holds the mortgage and promissory note) is not affected by the terms of the divorce decree, because their commitment to the mortgagee predates the divorce and remains intact even after the divorce is final. This is why refinancing is often required.

What happens if refinancing cannot occur? This is not an unusual circumstance. Mortgage lending requirements have gotten tighter, and sometimes one person can no longer qualify on his or her own for a new mortgage. On a more individual note, divorce can be tough on a person's credit rating, especially if late payments happened during the divorce process or the couple went through a foreclosure or bankruptcy as a part of the divorce. If one (or both) of you has experienced credit blight as a result, it can be very hard to qualify individually for a mortgage. Most lenders want to see the credit rating restored over a period of time (several months or years), through timely payments on existing debt.

It is important to know whether refinancing can be obtained *prior* to the finalization of divorce. This is not something you want dropped in your lap after the fact. If refinancing cannot happen, then you'll need to decide whether the property will be sold (to eliminate the mortgage and promissory note) or whether the person awarded the property will simply be required to service the existing debt on a timely basis. If the debt is simply to be serviced, as opposed to selling the property, then provisions are put into place to protect the other spouse. For example, my documents require the home to be immediately sold or refinanced if the spouse awarded the property falls behind a month or more in making the mortgage payments.

If refinancing cannot immediately occur, then the spouse who was not awarded the property needs to consider two issues. First, can the spouse who retains the property be trusted to make timely payments on the existing mortgage? And second, can the nonowner spouse obtain a mortgage while remaining on the existing mortgage, even though it is being serviced by the other person? It used to be relatively easy for the nonowner spouse to qualify for a separate mortgage as long as the spouse who retained the property was ordered by the terms of the judgment and decree to service the original mortgage. But this is no longer always the case.

Many lenders will not extend additional financing to the nonowner spouse if they are obligated under the terms of an existing mortgage. So, if you do not trust your ex-spouse, or you want to purchase property and cannot obtain financing because of an existing mortgage, then you want the property to be sold and the current mortgage(s) to be extinguished. Plain and simple.

Now, let's take a breath.

DIVIDING UP RETIREMENT PLANS

In addition to real property, any interest awarded in retirement monies will have to be divided. If the retirement interest is in an IRA (individual retirement account), the only thing usually necessary to divide the asset is paperwork, which is most commonly filled out and submitted by the spouse who is the owner of the IRA. Often, a certified copy of the judgment and decree is also required to be submitted along with the paperwork.

A qualified retirement benefit under ERISA (Employee's Retirement Income Security Act), such as a defined contribution plan (like a 401(k)), or a defined benefit plan (like a pension), must be divided by what's known as a either domestic relations order (DRO) or a qualified domestic relations order (QDRO). A QDRO is a court order and is usually drafted by one of the individual's attorneys after the divorce is completed. It specifies how the qualified retirement plan is to be divided between the now-divorced people. Once it is drafted, the proposed QDRO is submitted to the retirement plan's plan administrator for pre-approval, and once it is approved, the QDRO is then sent for review and signature to the district court judge who signed the original judgment and decree. Once the judge signs the document, and it is filed with the court administrator, then one of the attorneys secures a certified copy of the QDRO and sends it to the plan administrator for implementation. From that point forward, the retirement plan is divided according to the terms of the QDRO.

DEBT

After divorce, it is not uncommon for people to divide up debt, especially credit card debt. I've seen where one person will take over the payments on a joint credit card, and continue to make payments until the debt is retired. A better idea, however, is that whoever takes on the debt should roll it on to a credit card in his or her name only. Why? To extinguish the possibility of credit blight for the person who was not ordered to service the debt. If the debt remains in the names of both people, then each person's credit is dinged if payments are not made on a timely basis, or if the person ordered to service the debt defaults entirely on the debt. Just like with the homestead mortgage and promissory note, the debt to the credit card company precedes—and is not affected by—the terms of the judgment and decree.

So, your spouse may be ordered to pay the joint debt to ABC Credit Card, but if he or she stops paying the debt, rest assured the credit card company will come after you in an attempt to try and collect it. If the company successfully collects the debt against you, then your recourse is to take your spouse to court and try to get him ordered to reimburse you for the payment of the debt. What a pain! But that's the way it works.

DO (OR REDO) YOUR ESTATE PLAN

I suggest to all of my clients that they create or revise their estate plans after their divorces are completed. While under the terms of the summons, you cannot change your estate plan (or the beneficiaries of your life insurance, retirement plans, and bank accounts), unless you have the permission of either the court or your spouse. After the divorce, you can (and should!) do so. With regard to many assets you may be awarded (like pay on death—POD—assets, such as life insurance, and some retirement plans and bank accounts), this is as straightforward as changing the beneficiary information.

Your estate plan should be as simple or complex as your estate. For many people, all that is necessary is: 1) creating a simple will that specifies who gets what when you die; 2) changing the beneficiary designations on your POD assets; 3) making a health care directive (this document tells your health care providers what kinds of medical intervention you want if you cannot speak for yourself, and appoints a health care agent to act in your stead); and 4) perhaps drafting a power of attorney, which would allow someone to manage your affairs if you were to become incapacitated. The estate planning does not need to cost a lot of money, and the same attorney (or firm) who handled your divorce may be able to complete it for you.

MISCELLANEOUS (VEHICLE TITLES, PERSONAL PROPERTY, NAME CHANGE)

Other miscellaneous clean-up work includes changing titles to certain assets, which can usually be done by the individuals themselves, without the help of their attorneys. Occasionally, people will have to divide up personal property (like household goods and furnishings) after the divorce. This process, too, is often managed without the assistance of counsel. Some people, usually women, change their name as a part of divorce. This generally involves bringing certified copies of the divorce decree to the department of motor vehicles (DMV), the Social Security Administration, the bank, and any place else where you may have to show evidence of your legal name change (think voter registration or changing the name on your credit card).

Emotional Clean-Up

In addition to the postdivorce legal issues that require attention, there are emotional issues that also need consideration.

What do I mean by this?

Well, for example, when your spouse comes to pick up the children for parenting time, do you let him come into your home to greet and retrieve the children? Or would you prefer for him to wait outside (or maybe even in the car)?

What happens when a member of your ex-spouse's family, to whom you were close (say your former mother-in-law), dies? Do you go to her funeral? Or do the children attend the funeral with your ex, while you send flowers and a card instead? Do you and your ex continue to go to the children's school conferences together? Say you and your ex-spouse both participate in the same service organization. Do you continue to jointly participate, or does one of you bow out gracefully from that commitment?

Truly, there are no "right" answers to these questions, other than what is right for you, that is. But these issues require some thought, preferably forethought, because no one likes to be caught off guard or embarrassed.

I have had clients whose choices land all over the spectrum. Some of my clients have continued to celebrate holidays and birthdays jointly with their children. Some of my clients meet their ex-spouses at a mutually convenient location to exchange the children because they do not want their ex on the premises of their new homes. Some clients continue to serve on the same church committees together, while others choose to communicate only in writing. My clients are all different, and their needs can change over time. The boundaries that served them well right after the divorce may no longer be necessary five years later.

Whatever your needs may be, make sure you articulate them. If you would prefer that your ex-spouse not enter your new home when she comes to pick up the children, then communicate this (outside of the earshot of the children, of course). You can create new procedures and protocols with your ex-spouse, and you do not need to continue to be the person you were in your marriage. You can change up the game!

I also want to take a moment to touch on the subject of joint friends of the divorced couple. You may find that after your divorce, some (or many) of your couple friends no longer call or choose to interact with you (or your spouse) now that you're "singletons." This can be very painful for some of my clients, and it seems to happen quite frequently. I'm not sure why, but I suspect that the divorce of friends who are a couple may call into question the state of the marriages of their other couple friends. Many people resist looking at the status of their own marriages, and certainly don't want the divorce of their coupled friends to "spread" or be "caught" among the other couples. I also believe that the couple friends want to refrain from choosing sides in the divorce, and often steer away completely from both divorcing people.

In addition to creating new boundaries and navigating new roads in existing relationships, divorce can also be a time for deep personal introspection and change. We will talk about this in-depth in the next chapter, but consider this is a good time to get some advice from a seasoned professional, whether it be a counselor, a coach, or perhaps a pastor. It can be hard to make sense of divorce, sift through the lessons, and contemplate what may be next.

What's next for you?

- Make a list of the legal items (real property, retirement accounts, titles, and so forth) that you'll need to "clean up." Put those things into a calendar, giving yourself the space to take one at a time without feeling overwhelmed.

- Have you kindly articulated to your ex what your needs are as far as personal boundaries and communication are concerned? If not, now is a good time to take care of yourself so that you don't get caught off guard.

- Now that your divorce is finalized, how are you getting support and counsel? If you're not doing so yet, consider how having someone neutral to talk to would help open up your processing space and make more room for healing.

Divorce as an Opportunity for Growth and Transformation

Reclaiming Your Personal Power and Creating Life Anew

Perhaps more than any other life transition, other than death, divorce ushers in the greatest opportunity to change one's inner and outer landscapes.

Often the externals change, regardless. Divorcing people have to square up to and resolve such issues as creating parenting time arrangements for their kids, dividing assets and liabilities, and selling the homestead and relocating.

Divorce is also a time for potent internal change—if you so choose. Some of my clients don't want to touch personal growth with a ten-foot pole, while others embrace it.

To speak candidly, I am concerned about the folks who do not choose to use divorce as an opportunity for self-reflection and change. I have seen too many of them repeat the same mistakes—and end up back in my office. I call these folks "frequent flyers." Their reticence to grow personally seems to book them on the same flight, in the same seat, again and again and again.

I think divorce is particularly primed for personal growth, because it often coincides with the proverbial midlife crisis. At this time, the rules by which life is lived seem to change, as Swiss psychologist, Carl Jung, noted:

> Thoroughly unprepared, we take the step into the afternoon of life. Worse still, we take this step with the false presupposition that our truths and our ideals will serve us as hitherto. But we cannot live the afternoon of life according to the program of life's morning, for what was great in the morning will be little at evening and what in the morning was true, at evening will have become a lie.[1]

Let's take a typical example. Say Sarah met Tim in college. They dated in school, and then afterward, each of them began their careers. After a few years of dating, they got married at age twenty-six. Then, a couple of years later, the kids came—two of them. Three years apart.

For Sarah and Tim, the early years of their marriage were filled with ambition and the donning of certain roles—establishing their careers, getting married, and becoming spouses and parents. This was also a period of acquiring things and experiences—buying that first home or a new car, taking trips, and so forth. This is generally not the time for individual personal growth for either spouse. Their commitments related to marriage, children, work, and social connection practically ensured that Sarah and Tim did not come up for air, let alone reflection, for several years.

Self-reflection and personal growth tend to be hotter topics a little later on in life, and at times of big transitions. The end of a marriage (especially one that has had some years on it), coupled with being over the age of forty (when the shadow of mortality begins to loom in the background), often leads my clients to ask: "Who am I and what am I going to do with the time that I have left?"

Many clients, especially women, are stepping out of roles they have played, and which have defined them, for decades. Some openly wonder, "Who am I if I'm not someone's wife or a mother with children who are still at home? Who am I if I no longer live in Green Acres or the home I've been in for twenty years?"

This is why I always recommend therapy or coaching for my clients. I can help them navigate the legal divorce, which, as I've said, is at its heart just a business transaction. But again, the emotional divorce, the why, is the most important piece of the dissolution pie.

At first blush, the why of divorce can appear superficially easy to discern.

"He cheated on me."

"She left."

"He's a drunk."

"She loves her job more than she loves me."

These "causes," however, are almost never the instigators of the divorce. Rather, they are almost always the outer effects of deep-seated issues that have festered for a long time between the marriage partners.

Often, these issues reflect unspoken expectations in the relationship. Many couples don't have the hard conversations. I commonly hear stories from clients that many of the issues fundamental to the relationship were never addressed, like money management, whether they planned to have children (and, if so, how many and when), or if the relationship was going to be monogamous or not.

Turns out, silence is not golden—at least not with respect to marital expectations. Silence on these important issues can be a predictor of marital doom. In fact, whole books have been devoted to how best to flesh out these expectations, through important, and sometimes difficult, conversations.

One core, implied expectation that I regularly see among my clients or their spouses is an expectation that someone or something else (their spouses, their children, their jobs, or their possessions) is responsible for both their experience of life and their happiness. This is a misplacement of personal responsibility! It makes it very easy for this person to blame their spouse or the situation, generally, rather than using the opportunity to evaluate their own needs, their own feelings, and their own behaviors.

As a seasoned divorce attorney, I can now spot this projection a mile away. When I ask what led them to divorce, I'll hear responses that reassign responsibility. For example, "I cheated on my spouse," gets translated into, "She cut me off," or, "He did things that made me not feel close to him." With regard to money, "I overspent repeatedly and incurred substantial debt," is told to me as, "He micromanaged me, including my spending." In a recent example, "My wife's just jealous," turned into the revelation that my client had a girlfriend for the last five years of his marriage.

In my experience, folks who blame and who make their spouses "the bad guy," while claiming "the good guy" label for themselves, are in for trouble. The unwillingness to be personally responsible for their contributions to the demise of the marriage (and it always takes two to tango) means that the likelihood of them repeating these same patterns in a new relationship is high. Why? Because the behaviors, as well as their underlying causes, have not been identified, let alone worked on or changed.

According to the late Debbie Ford, author of *Spiritual Divorce: Divorce as a Catalyst for an Extraordinary Life*, we pick partners with the same level of woundedness as our own.[2] In other words, twos don't end up with tens and tens don't end up with twos! Rather, there is always parity between the partners in a marriage relationship. What we hate about our spouse is really what we hate about ourselves! Our spouses are just convenient mirrors for our own reflection and learning. Blame deflects the analysis away from the parts of us that we hide from ourselves and judge, and places the focus, instead, on the parts of our spouse that we despise and criticize! After all, it's easier for us to accuse than admit, isn't it?

The biggest opportunity for personal transformation in divorce is the reclamation of personal responsibility for our lives. Even if our spouses abused us or our children, we still have to own the fact that we selected this person as a marriage partner and likely tolerated unacceptable behavior from them for way too long. Again, I am not saying that any of this is easy! Or that it comes without having to deal with a lot of guilt and shame! But, "[e]ven if I can't see how I did it, or why I did it," says Ford, "the very fact that this problem is in my life tells me that I have participated in its creation."[3]

Reclaiming personal responsibility means no longer looking for outside causes for our feelings. There is tremendous power and healing in this. We're no longer giving our power away to someone else. Once we own our power, we can begin to look at the unhealed emotional wounds that contributed to the demise of our marriages. "Our anger, bitterness, grief, fear, guilt, and shame drive us to behaviors that sabotage our happiness," says Ford.[4] When we understand how we sabotage our own happiness, we have the ability to cleanse the underlying wounds, which will enable us to make different choices going forward. Making different choices on a go-forward basis will completely change both the circumstances, and the experiences, of our lives.

If there is a silver lining in going through a divorce, perhaps this is it: we can use the experience to change ourselves and create life anew—a life with new relationships to ourselves and to others, which are happier, more peaceful, and more loving.

Forgiveness

When my clients ask me about what "required reading" I would recommend during their divorce, I always mention Dr. Fred Luskin's book *Forgive for Good: A Proven Prescription for Health and Happiness*. Dr. Luskin is the cofounder and the director of the Stanford University Forgiveness Project, and conducts an ongoing series of workshops and research related to forgiveness.

As a part of his research, Dr. Luskin found that the practice of forgiveness reduces anger, hurt, depression, and stress. And furthermore, forgiveness leads to healthier relationships, as well as better physical health. Forgiveness is also capable of positively enhancing our attitudes, which opens up the heart to kindness, beauty, and love.[5]

During and after divorce, each person needs to process and release feelings of anger, hurt, depression, and stress. Even if the divorce was "amicable," there is still a huge loss of the dreams that were possible for the couple at the outset of marriage. And no one wants to go through divorce again, so the idea of completing the inner work to facilitate healthier future relationships is important. Even if you decide to never get married again, the benefit of being more open to kindness, beauty, and love is life-enhancing and worth embracing.

Before we get into the mechanics of forgiveness, I think we need to define what forgiveness means, as well as identify the types of forgiveness. There are two definitions of forgiveness I like. The first is that forgiveness is giving up the hope that the past could have been any different. (I am not sure who said that originally, but a very similar quote has been attributed to Lily Tomlin: "Forgiveness means giving up all hope for a better past.") The second definition I like comes from Dr. Luskin himself, and can be summarized as follows: forgiveness does not mean forgetting or reconciling. Forgiveness means finding peace and understanding so that you can feel better, heal, and move forward.

There are also two types of forgiveness that fall in line with these definitions, both of which are equally important. The first type of forgiveness is referred to by Dr. Luskin as interpersonal forgiveness, which means forgiving someone else or even, perhaps, the situation.

The other type of forgiveness, which can be even harder to implement than interpersonal forgiveness, is self-forgiveness. So, forgiveness work needs to be done on both sides of the equation: us *and* them.

So is there a process for forgiving?

Indeed there is!

According to Dr. Luskin, there are three components to both interpersonal forgiveness and self-forgiveness. They include: 1) taking things less personally; 2) taking responsibility for your feelings; and 3) telling a positive intention story.[6] Let's talk about each of these individually.

TAKING THINGS LESS PERSONALLY

When I first started practicing in the area of divorce, my mentor, Ann Schulz, made a comment about our clients and their spouses that has stuck with me through the years. Ann said: "It's been a long time since a perfect person walked the face of the earth."

She meant the comment somewhat tongue-in-cheek, and I laughed; but I recognized the statement as truth. We are all human beings and we can be "human failings" at times. We have all made mistakes. We have all been unkind. And every mistake is one that has been made before. A thousand times before. A million times before. Your spouse did not invent betrayal or addiction. You did not pioneer the feelings of hurt, shame, or resentment. No! Taking things less personally means recognizing that we all make mistakes (huge ones at times), and that it is a *choice* to forgive, learn, and grow, as opposed to staying stuck and continuing to beat ourselves (or the other person or situation) up.

TAKING RESPONSIBILITY FOR YOUR FEELINGS

One of my favorite quotes by Dr. Luskin is: "Difficulties, mistreatments and unkindness do not have an extended warranty."[7] How true! Ultimately, we are responsible for our emotional experience. Everyone has had unpleasant experiences in their past. Not everyone, though, regurgitates these experiences to ruin the present moment. If we give over our power to the person or event that hurt us, we become helpless. Instead, in order for our painful feelings to diminish, we must reclaim our power by being responsible for how we feel.

Dr. Luskin recommends two healing techniques when grappling with this issue. The first technique is the practice of gratitude—which is something we touched on in an earlier chapter. Even something as simple as writing down three things we are grateful for can change the focus of our perspective from pain and blame to beauty and love. The second technique is called PERT, or positive emotion refocusing technique. PERT is more fully described in Dr. Luskin's book and is a technique that takes about forty-five seconds to practice. Practicing PERT allows us to stay in control of our emotions and takes away the power of other people to hurt us. The technique involves deep breathing, bringing an image of something or someone we love to mind, and then, once relaxed, asking the now-peaceful part of us what we can do to resolve our difficulty.[8] I have used PERT myself and have found it to be very beneficial when I am off on a "blame run," or when I am otherwise giving my power away.

TELLING A POSITIVE INTENTION STORY

Telling a positive intention story means becoming the hero, instead of the victim, in the stories we tell to others and to ourselves. In the typical grievance story, where we cast ourselves as the victim, the focus is on telling and retelling the offense committed by the other person (or by ourselves), as well as how badly we feel about it. What these stories truly reflect is an unwillingness to cope. Both continuing to feel as though we have been wronged, and remaining stuck in the guilt of having wronged another, have the same payoff. These feelings preserve a cycle of stagnancy, and they keep us from changing.

Dr. Luskin relates this story about Donna. Now, Donna's story is so universal that she could have been any one of my divorce clients or their spouses. Her seventeen-year marriage had been in trouble for a long while. Donna's husband worked all the time and traveled frequently, and she was alone a lot. Their sex life was nonexistent. Donna was also approaching midlife. Her children were teenagers and would soon be moving out and getting on with their own lives.

Donna's marriage ended with an affair—her own—with her husband's friend. Donna felt a tremendous amount of guilt about having had an affair, ending her marriage, and hurting the children. She decided that having an affair meant that the end of the marriage was solely her fault, despite the fact that there was longstanding marital discord. Donna's guilt over the affair, and her inability to forgive herself, resulted in a sort of emotional paralysis in moving forward with a new relationship (which was not with the lover, and which she ended at the same time she ended her marriage).

Dr. Luskin writes:

> Donna's positive intention was to create a successful long-term relationship. She did not want to give up on marriage just because her first had ended badly. Donna saw that she had to learn better communication skills to avoid the problems that occurred in her marriage to Jeff. She understood that she was not assertive enough with Jeff and that she had fooled herself into thinking things would magically get better. After her divorce, Donna decided that a new relationship would have to wait. She saw with some chagrin that she was capable of unkind actions such as having an affair. Therefore, she took it upon herself to develop new parts of herself with a therapist. She wanted to learn about herself and thereby grow in the hope of creating a stronger relationship with another man.[9]

Donna's positive intention was to create a successful long-term relationship. She became the hero of this story by deciding to learn from the failure of her first marriage and to consciously grow into the person who would be capable of sustaining a healthy, functional relationship.

Forgiveness in the context of divorce may seem like a tall order. But it is doable, and until you choose to forgive, you will not be truly free to move forward with your new life. And life is good on the other side of forgiveness! Better emotional health. Better physical health. Better relationships. More beauty. More kindness. More love.

Forgive for (your own) good.

Dreaming New Dreams and Navigating Your Way to Them

For many people, it's hard to know which way is up after going through divorce. Dreams have been shattered. There's debris all over the place. You may hurt. Your kids may hurt. Life has changed, and, in your opinion, not for the better.

For others, divorce is liberating. The pain of the divorce pales in comparison to the pain, discomfort, or boredom they endured during the marriage. For them, the joy of life is quickly restored, and new dreams and opportunities abound.

Whether you fall into either of these groups—or somewhere in between—the truth is that divorce is always a doorway, a threshold, to a whole new life. This new life is what you make it. It's up to you. You can make your life happy, exciting, and joyful—or not. As Henry Ford once said, "Whether you think you can, or you think you can't—you're right."

I am going to presume that you would like your life to be happier, more exciting, and more joyful. I am also going to assume that you're open to looking at where you can take your life, and what dreams still live inside you that desire to be expressed.

The first stop in navigating this road is to take an inventory, both of how your life is at this very moment and what your idealized life would look like. In coaching, this exercise is referred to as the Wheel of Life, and looks like this:

There are six segments to the wheel. The first part of the inventory is to rate your current life satisfaction. You rate each segment on a scale from one to ten, with one being the lowest ranking, and ten being the highest. As a part of this inventory, I think it is also helpful to make notes to accompany the rankings. What makes one segment rank so low? What makes another segment rank so high? In other words, it is important to identify the reasons behind the ranking.

Why? Because when you identify the specific things in your life that need to change, as well as identify what areas need further enhancement, you'll realize just how much they contribute to your enjoyment of life.

The second part of the inventory focuses on dreaming. What would make each segment a ten out of ten? For this part of the inventory, I encourage you to be wild and to think about what your life would both look and feel like if you had a magic wand and could instantaneously make each piece of the pie into your highest ideal. Think outside of the box. Be unbridled. Be wholly creative. Be fearless.

Your willingness to envision your wildest, highest, and best vision for your life is imperative to creating a new life. Why? Because possibility begins with imagination. Also, this part of the inventory will tell you what is really important to you. It gives you a vision for how life—at its very best—would be for you. And without a vision, says the Bible, the people perish. And so, too, for us as individuals, I believe.

How do we close the gap between what our lives are like currently and the life the way we would ideally like it to be? Well, Greg S. Reid, the American filmmaker, motivational speaker, and best-selling author (of The Napoleon Hill Foundation's Think and Grow Rich book series) says this in one of his widely circulated motivational speeches: "A dream written down with a date becomes a goal. A goal broken down into steps becomes a plan. A plan backed by action makes your dreams come true."[10]

Writing down your goals and taking action to support them are important. To take it a step further, public commitment and accountability are also fundamental, and greatly increase the likelihood of success. Dr. Gail Matthews, from the Dominican University of California, has conducted research that shows that people who write their goals down, and who enlist friends to hold them accountable by sending them weekly progress reports, succeed in achieving their goals approximately 75 percent of the time. Given this, Dr. Matthews suggests the three elements to goal achievement are: 1) writing your goals down, 2) making a public commitment to your goals (such as to your friends/family), and 3) external accountability (like to your friends/family) via weekly progress reports.[11]

There is also research to support the role of affirmations ("I can do this") and positivity in the achievement of goals. Apparently, positivity is the key to goal achievement, because, just like gratitude, it enables you to deal with stress more effectively. Affirmations are also integral to goal achievement because they tend to help you control your impulses and keep the focus positive and vision oriented.

Oliver Wendell Holmes, Sr. said: "Many people die with their music still in them. Why is this so? Too often it is because they are always getting ready to live. Before they know it, time runs out." Don't die with your music still in you! Follow and actualize your dreams by writing them down, publicly acknowledging them, and being regularly accountable to someone else for your progress. The only thing standing between you and your goals and dreams is *you*.

Adult Attachment Theory: Knowing the Science Behind Attraction

What is this subject doing in a book about divorce? Well, if you don't want to get divorced again, you will definitely want to read this section. Adult attachment theory may well be the most important key to creating a healthy, functional marriage. It may also expose the underlying problem in most marriages that end in divorce.

Before I begin discussing this issue in detail, I want to acknowledge an excellent, well-researched book, which I read cover to cover in preparing to write this section. The book is *Attached: The New Science of Adult Attachment and How It Can Help You Find—and Keep—Love*, by Amir Levine, MD and Rachel S. F. Heller, MA. I highly recommend it to anyone who has additional interest in this subject matter.[12]

Adult attachment theory focuses on the ways that people perceive and respond to intimacy in romantic relationships. There are three main attachment styles: *secure*, *anxious*, and *avoidant*.

About 50 percent of the population is securely attached. Those with a secure attachment style are warm, loving, and comfortable with intimacy.

Approximately 20 percent of the population has an anxious attachment style. People with an anxious attachment style desperately desire intimacy, but worry continually about their relationships and their partner's ability to love them.

Nearly 25 percent of the population has an avoidant attachment style. Adults with an avoidant attachment style want intimacy—but only at a distance—because they fear losing their independence.

The remaining 3 to 5 percent fall into a fourth, less common category. This category is a combination of both anxious and avoidant attachment styles.

How do you find out your attachment style? Well, you could read *Attached*. There is an attachment style inventory in the book. Otherwise, you can probably go online and find additional resources. You may even know intuitively what your attachment style is after reading this section.

Perhaps not surprisingly, people with different attachment styles have different needs with respect to intimacy and togetherness. They also approach the subjects of conflict, sex, and communication from different angles. And they also, generally speaking, have different expectations about their partners and their relationships.

In *Attached*, the authors point out that the knowledge of attachment styles can be an easy and reliable way to both comprehend and forecast behavior in romantic relationships. As it turns out, one's attachment style results in predictable, preprogrammed responses in coupling.

Securely attached people trust themselves and their environments. They are able to easily articulate their needs through effective communication.

Anxiously attached folks feel insecure in their relationship, and deal with their insecurity by being hypervigilant about their partner and their relationships. Anxiously attached people want to stay very close to their partners, and are often branded as "clingy" or "needy." When their needs are not met, those with anxious attachment styles often use what is known as *protest behavior*. I call it acting out. In any event, they act out to get their needs met. Often, the protest behavior has nothing to do with the real need that is going unmet. In other words, an argument over taking out the trash may really be due to the underlying need of the anxious partner to feel supported in the relationship.

Finally, those with avoidant attachment styles are uncomfortable being too close to others and often find it difficult to depend upon someone else. When someone gets to close, they employ deactivating strategies, which are behaviors or thoughts that are used to squelch intimacy and disengage from their partners.

Ideally, both those with anxious and avoidant attachment styles would end up with securely attached partners. Why? Because people with anxious and avoidant attachment styles become more secure in relationship with someone who is securely attached! The securely attached person values the needs of the partner as importantly as his or her own needs. So, the person with an anxious attachment style gets his or her needs for closeness and intimacy readily met by a securely attached partner without having to resort to protest behavior. A securely attached person is also able to value the independence of a partner with an avoidant attachment style, while still providing closeness and intimacy on a mutually acceptable basis.

But guess what? People with anxious and avoidant attachment styles are not initially attracted to someone with a secure attachment style. Rather, those who have anxious and avoidant attachment styles are often attracted to each other. This is what the authors of *Attached* refer to as the *anxious-avoidant trap*.

The anxious-avoidant trap is a collision between two people with vastly different relationship needs. Their union is likely to be turbulent, as opposed to a safe harbor for each. I can tell you that I see this dysfunctional pairing so often that I believe it must be a predictor for divorce.

The partner who is anxiously attached craves intimacy, while the partner with an avoidant attachment style feels uncomfortable when things become too close. Neither party is secure in the relationship. Rather, both parties are trapped in a vicious cycle of exacerbating their respective insecurities. The anxious partner may want to be exclusive, move in together, or get married. The avoidant partner may want to see other people, maintain separate residences, and avoid formal commitments. Further, the anxious partner is often the one who makes concessions in the relationship, accepting the "rules" imposed by the avoidant partner, all in an attempt to keep the relationship, and access to some amount of intimacy and closeness, alive. Sound familiar?

Here is what was most stunning to me: both attachment styles, and especially those who are anxious, misinterpret the activation of their attachment styles for "the spark" or "chemistry" or "passion" with a prospective partner. In order words, feeling inexorably drawn to someone can be a big red flag that you have met someone with an incompatible attachment style. Those with avoidant attachment styles often experience this in a slightly different way. They often pine for the "phantom ex" who was "the one who got away" or they may wax poetic about their future "soul mate," who has yet to appear.

In contrast, people with both anxious and avoidant attachment styles tend to feel calm in the presence of a securely attached partner. The messages from someone with a secure attachment are sincere, straightforward, and consistent. These folks feel worthy of love and are not afraid of intimacy. They don't engage in games, beat around the bush, or play hard to get. They also communicate their needs and desires well. Mixed messages, tension, and suspense go out the door. Yet, sometimes this can be experienced as boredom or indifference by someone with an anxious or avoidant attachment style, who expects bells, whistles, heavenly choruses, or rainbows in their wine to anoint the appearance of "the one."

Here's the great news. If someone with an anxious or an avoidant attachment style can reframe boredom and indifference for what it really is (care, concern, and availability), then their likelihood for success and happiness in a relationship goes up exponentially. A person with an insecure attachment (whether anxious or avoidant), who forms a relationship with someone securely attached, has a better functioning, less conflicted, and more highly satisfying union. Why? The secure partner acts as a buffer and nurtures their partner into a more secure and highly functioning position in the relationship.

Why does this matter if I am divorced?

It matters because it is highly likely that you will not remain single forever! You will go on to have other relationships, and, if you desire having a future relationship that is loving, nurturing, and functional, then a little knowledge of attachment theory can help you get there!

How to Effectively Love and Feel Loved in a New Relationship: The Five Love Languages

A little knowledge of the five love languages can also help you form a loving, nurturing, and functional relationship. Though you might already be familiar with the five love languages, I want to take a moment to introduce to this concept if it's new to you. Even if you're aware of the it, you may choose to read this section to refresh your recollection about the subject.

The 5 Love Languages: The Secret to Love That Lasts is a book written by Dr. Gary Chapman. He is both a pastor and a marriage counselor in North Carolina. Over several decades of counseling, Dr. Chapman realized that couples do not necessarily experience love in the same way. Some people feel loved by spending quality time with their spouse. Others feel nurtured by an act of service (think taking out the trash).[13]

Without being conscious of it, people tend to give love in their own primary love language (the way in which they best experience love), *not* in their partner's primary love language. Because of this, Dr. Chapman suggests that the secret to lasting love is to ask for love from your spouse in your primary love language, and to express love to your spouse in his or her primary love language.

When you're equipped with this information, you can fill your spouses "Love Tank" and he or she can fill yours with the actions that correspond to your respective primary love languages.

So what are the five love languages, anyway? They are:

1. **WORDS OF AFFIRMATION**—If this is your love language, you feel most cared for when your partner is open and expressive in telling you how wonderful they think you are, how much they appreciate you, and so forth.

2. **ACTS OF SERVICE**—If your partner's offer to watch the kids so you can go to the gym (or relieving you of some other task), makes your heart sing, then this is your love language.

3. **AFFECTION**—A warm hug, a kiss, touch, and sexual intimacy make you feel most loved when this is your love language.

4. **QUALITY TIME**—This love language is about being together, fully present and engaged in the activity at hand, no matter how trivial.

5. **GIFTS**—This is your love language if you feel acknowledged and seen by your partner's willingness to think about, acquire, and present a gift to you.

Some people know, intuitively, what their primary love language is. Others may not have a clue. Dr. Chapman has a five love languages test which you can use to assess what your love languages are. In determining your love languages, Dr. Chapman notes that your upbringing has a lot of influence on them. How did your parents show you love? In which ways did you feel most loved as a child? These questions and the answers to these questions will likely point to your primary love language.

It may also be possible to determine your primary love language by looking at what you do when you really want to show someone you care about them. Do you bring them a gift? Then your primary love language might be gifts. Do you want to take them out to dinner and spend time with them? Then your primary love language could be quality time.

Sometimes, even relationship heartaches can be telling as to your primary love language. If you feel badly hurt by someone close to you, pay attention to how this person did not show you love or nurturing in the way you wanted. In other words, the way in which they failed to nurture or love you is likely your primary love language.

It helps to know your top two love languages, as well as your least important love language. Why? Because some days, a warm hug (say affection is your second love language) can feel a lot better than the knowledge that your spouse put away the dishes (say acts of service is your primary love language). And if you know that gifts are on the bottom rung of your spouse's love languages ladder, then you can devote your efforts to the top one or two rungs instead.

I've included this material because this is not information most of us learned in school. While this is a book on divorce, I know that the vast majority of divorcing people will go on to have new relationships after they are divorced. In creating this new relationship, I think knowing how you best receive or experience love is important. I also believe that if you want your new partner to feel loved, one way of doing so is to learn their love languages, and then choose to nurture their primary ones.

Trusting Again After Divorce

You have just gotten divorced. You're not even thinking about dating again, let alone falling in love and trusting another human being with your heart!

This is the way the majority of my clients feel immediately after the divorce is done. For most people, however, this feeling doesn't last forever. They go on to date again, and many will remarry, in time.

Given this, it seems like a good idea to talk about the concept of trust, which is often decimated in the process of divorce. I want to define what trust is, and discuss the components that comprise it.

The definition of trust is the firm belief in the reliability, truth, ability, or strength of someone or something. Sounds like something you would definitely want to feel about a future partner, right? Most people who have gone through divorce have had their trust in their partner shattered. So, how to rebuild trust in a different relationship? What do you need to look for? What components should be present?

In preparation for this section of the book, I read a lot about trust. As I did, I began to see a repeating theme. Most of the information pointed to four elements that comprise trust.

The model I am going to refer to comes from the great book *Trust Works! Four Keys to Building Lasting Relationships*, by Kenneth Blanchard, with Cynthia Olmstead and Marcia Lawrence. In this book, the authors set forth the ABCD Trust Model.[14]

In this model, the *A* stands for *able*. This means that your partner must demonstrate competence. In the business setting, this is an easy element to identify: Can the employee do the job or not? But, what does this mean in an intimate relationship? To me, it means that the person you're dating shows up and fulfills your expectations. They are able to meet your articulated needs, and they choose to do so. In other words, their walk matches their talk.

B stands for *believable*. Simply put, the person you're dating is authentic, honest, and acts with integrity. By integrity, I mean the quality of possessing and steadfastly adhering to high moral principles. Said differently, they have values and live by them.

C stands for *connected*. The person you date should care about you and others, including those who are in your inner circle. They take your best interests to heart, and your well-being is just as important to them as their own. Connectedness includes being courteous and forgiving. It also includes valuing and nurturing the connection through good communication. Good communication hinges on the ability to be vulnerable. Being vulnerable again can be tough after divorce, but it is made easier if you feel respected and encouraged when you share. The person you date should be able to easily provide this safe space for you, and you should feel comfortable doing so as well.

Finally, *D* stands for *dependable*. Being dependable means being reliable, accountable, and consistent. Does the person you're dating keep the promises he or she makes? Is he accountable for his actions? Does she send the same message to you consistently? Or does the message change, depending upon the audience, or the mood, or the time of day? The predictability of the person you're dating increases the sense of safety you feel in the relationship.

I think it is important to note that trust is a process. It doesn't rise and fall on one incident or conversation. It is a pattern that reveals itself over time. Step-by-step. Date by date. You'll know.

Perhaps this is the most important aspect of re-establishing trust: you'll need to trust yourself again. To this end, I think these same principles apply to how you treat yourself. Can you articulate and meet your own needs (able)? Can you believe in yourself? Are you authentic, honest, and in integrity, both with yourself and with others? Are you connected to yourself? Do you know what your needs and values are? Do you have your own best interests at heart? Are you good at communicating your needs and meeting them? Can you be vulnerable and forgiving? Can you depend upon yourself? Do you keep the promises you make to yourself? Can you rely on yourself to take actions that are in alignment with your needs, dreams, and values? If you can answer these questions affirmatively, then you have done a good job at rebuilding your own trust.

Well, we've come to the end of our road together. Again, I realize that none of this—from the first thought that your marriage may be in trouble, all the way up to the entry of your final judgment and decree (and beyond)—is easy. It never is. Even if you want to be divorced, it can still be an unsettling, scary, and painful process.

How you get through the process, is, in large measure, up to you. You may not be able to control all of the circumstances that affect your divorce, but you certainly do control your responses to them.

When you think about how you're going to respond, I ask you to remember what we discussed in the preface. Divorce is a legal process that dissolves the bonds of matrimony and restructures the family into separate households. It does not dissolve the family! If you have kids, you're still going to have to figure out how to parent together, and you'll probably see your ex-spouse at every big family event (baptisms, weddings, funerals, or holidays). Even if you don't have kids, you may still see your ex frequently around town, keep in touch with his or her family, and interact with the same group of friends.

How do you want to experience all of this? And what about your children's experiences of the divorce and its aftermath? Do you want the collective experience to be one of anger, nastiness, retribution, judgment, and unforgiveness? Or something else?

Choosing the higher ground gives you a completely different panorama. You'll feel better—physical and emotionally—throughout the divorce and beyond. You'll make informed, well-reasoned decisions which reflect the needs, values, and preferences of both yourself and your family. You'll feel good about yourself and your decisions, irrespective of your spouse's choices and actions. And you'll be more ready for your new life after the divorce is concluded.

And this, in my opinion, is what it means to divorce wisely.

Acknowledgments

A book really doesn't get written by just the author herself. I am grateful to all of the following, without whom this handbook would not have seen the light of day.

To God: thank you for your unconditional and unwavering love and support of me throughout this project, and for your Grace. Thank you for the stamina and the drive to write this book, despite the many other demands of life, several of which took a back seat throughout this project. I acknowledge that there is no separation, that only love is real, and that we are all the beloved children of God, in whom you are well pleased.

To *A Course in Miracles*: thank you for helping me choose love over fear as a daily practice.

To my family and friends: thank you for loving me and supporting me throughout this project. Thank you for allowing me to follow my dreams without questioning or judgment.

To my colleagues at the firm: thank you for supporting me through out this process and for picking up the slack that was let out when I decided to write a book.

To my clients: thank you for allowing me the privilege of serving you and for sharing your hopes, dreams, and fears with me. I am honored and touched.

To my professional colleagues in Minnesota: thank you for helping our clients navigate the often difficult transition of divorce. Thank you for sharing your wisdom. It is an absolute pleasure to work with you.

To my editor, Lizzie Vance (lizzievance.com): thank you for getting this book banged into shape, and for your unwavering support throughout this project. Thank you for calming me, encouraging me, brainstorming with me, and being gentle with me. I so appreciate you, and couldn't have completed the book without you.

To Kelly Notaras and kn literary arts (knliterary.com): thank you for your support and for your wisdom in matching Lizzie Vance, Elisabeth Rinaldi, Beth Skelley, and Matt Klein to this project. I so appreciate it.

To my cover designer, Miladinka Milic (milagraphicartist.com): thank you for creating a beautiful and powerful cover design for this book.

To my photographer, Matt Seefeldt (seefeldtphoto.com): thank you for the fantastic photographs, which capture my essence *and* make me look about ten years younger and twenty pounds lighter!

To my proofreader, Elisabeth Rinaldi (inkypawediting.com): thank you for the most excellent spelling, grammar, and citation checking! I so appreciate your finishing touches on the book.

To my book layout designer, Beth Skelley: thank you for choosing an internal layout for the book that is approachable, professional, and stylish.

To Matt Klein: thank you for your marketing acumen and advice.

To Aaron Stephens, MBA: thank you for being a way-shower through this whole process. Thank you for your most excellent web, Twitter, and Facebook designs. Thank you for being an endless fount of knowledge and support, and for your willingness to share your journey with me.

To Mile Hi Church and Dr. Roger Teel: thank you for spiritually feeding me before, during, and after this process. I feel so blessed to have found my spiritual home.

Last, but certainly not least: thank you to my precious boxer, Scout, for always being at the ready with your wiggly little nub of a tail. Your loving presence raised my spirits more often than you will ever know.

Suzanne E. Grandchamp, Esq., 2015

Appendix A

Participation Agreement

COLLABORATIVE PROCESS PARTICIPATION AGREEMENT

I. PRINCIPLES, GOALS AND VALUES

A. We, the Participants, believe that it is in our best interests and the best interests of our minor children to reach an agreement re: **Marriage of First Middle Last and First Middle Last** through the Collaborative process rather than by going to Court.

B. The Collaborative process is based on:
- honesty (full and complete disclosure of all assets, debts and income);
- satisfying the interests of both participants;
- cooperation;
- integrity;
- professionalism;
- dignity; and
- respect.

C. The Collaborative process focuses on our **future** well-being and the future well-being of our children. To achieve this goal, we agree not to engage in unnecessary discussions of past events.

D. The Collaborative process does **not** rely on Court-imposed solutions.

E. Our goals are:
- to resolve our differences in the best interests of our children;
- to eliminate the negative economic, social and emotional consequences of litigation; and
- to find solutions that are acceptable to both of us.

F. **Commitment.** There is no guarantee we will succeed by using the Collaborative process. We understand that our success is primarily dependent upon our commitment to the process.

G. **Relational Concerns.** We understand that this process cannot eliminate concerns about any disharmony, distrust, or differences that have led to our marriage dissolution. Nevertheless addressing these concerns may be important to both of us. Therefore, we may jointly engage a coach (or each of us may engage our own coach) trained in Collaborative Practice, as set forth in Paragraph VII below, to assist us with these concerns so these concerns do not impede our progress.

H. **Therapeutic Needs.** This process is not designed to address therapeutic or psychological issues. When these or other non-legal issues arise, Collaborative professionals may refer us to appropriate experts or consultants. (See, paragraph VII for definition of "Collaborative professionals").

II. DISCLOSURE

A. We agree to disclose all information relevant to the issues that we must decide, whether requested or not. All requests for disclosure will be made informally, and we will respond promptly, candidly and completely. We will update information promptly whenever it materially changes.

B. By using informal discovery we are choosing not to use formal procedures and methods available in the traditional court process. We agree to use these informal measures with the specific understanding that, in return, we can rely on each other to make full and fair disclosure of all assets, income, debts and other information necessary for a fair settlement. We each may require the other to sign a sworn statement fully disclosing all assets, income, debts and other information. Participation in the Collaborative process, and the settlement reached, is based on our agreement to act in good faith and provide complete and accurate information to the best of our abilities.

III. BEGINNING AND CONCLUDING THE COLLABORATIVE PROCESS

We agree that the Collaborative process begins when we sign this agreement, and that it concludes (1) upon the resolution of the Collaborative matter(s) that may be evidenced by a Notice of Conclusion or such other ways as the parties may agree on, or (2) upon termination of this Collaborative process, as set forth in Paragraph XI below.

IV. PROCESS

A. **Out-of-Court.** We commit ourselves to settling this case without going to Court.

B. **Joint Meetings.** We agree to engage in informal discussions and conferences to settle all issues. All communication during joint meetings will focus on the property, financial, and parenting issues in the dissolution and the constructive resolution of those issues.

We may discuss issues with each other outside joint meetings if we both agree and are comfortable doing so. We also are free to insist that any discussions be reserved for the joint meetings where Collaborative professionals are present. We will not spring discussions on the other in unscheduled telephone calls or in surprise visits to the other's residence.

Costs for joint meetings are substantial and we agree to be fully prepared for each meeting.

C. **Legal Documents.** We will sign a Joint Petition at the beginning of this process unless the proceeding has been started by service of a Summons and Petition. The Joint Petition will not be filed with the Court until a full agreement is reached and the final documents have been signed. We will not file any motion or document that would initiate court intervention during the Collaborative process, except for any temporary agreement we reach and mutually agree to file. After we reach a final agreement, we will have our attorneys prepare the documents necessary to finalize our divorce.

V. WE WILL NEGOTIATE IN GOOD FAITH

A. **Good Faith Negotiation.** We understand that this process will involve good faith negotiation.

B. **Legal Issues.** The process is designed to resolve the following legal issues:
- Parenting time and decision making;
- Financial support of our children, including unreimbursed medical and dental expenses of our minor children, and child care costs, if any;
- Insurance (e.g., medical, dental, life);
- Spousal maintenance;
- Division of property and debts;
- Nonmarital property;
- Prenuptial agreements;
- Taxes;
- Attorney's fees and costs; and
- Other issues we may agree to address.

C. **Interest-based Negotiations.** We agree to negotiate based on interests and not positions.

D. **Balanced Approach.** We will be expected to take a balanced approach to resolving all differences. Where our interests differ, we will each use our best efforts to create proposals that are acceptable to both of us.

E. **Use of the Law.** None of us will use threats of litigation as a way of forcing settlement. We may, however, discuss the law and the likely outcome of going to Court.

F. **Negotiate with Integrity.** We will maintain a high standard of integrity. We shall not take advantage of any miscalculations or mistakes, but shall immediately identify and correct them.

G. **Attorney Role.** Although we pledge to be respectful and to negotiate in an interest-based manner, we are each entitled to assert our respective interests, and our attorneys will help us do this in a productive manner. We understand that each attorney has a professional duty to represent his or her own client diligently and is not the attorney for the other. This is so even though the attorneys share a commitment to the Collaborative process.

VI. CHILDREN'S ISSUES

A. We agree to act quickly to resolve differences related to our children.

B. We agree to promote a caring, loving, and involved relationship between our children and each parent.

C. We agree to work for the best interests of the family as a whole.

D. We agree not to involve our children in our differences.

E. We acknowledge that inappropriate communications regarding our dissolution can be harmful to our children. Communication with our children regarding the dissolution will occur only if it is appropriate and done by mutual agreement or with the advice of a neutral child specialist. We specifically agree that our children will not be included in any discussion regarding this process, except as described in this Agreement.

F. During this process, we each agree to notify the other parent if we travel with the children overnight and we will not change the residence of our children without the prior written consent of the other parent.

VII. COLLABORATIVE TEAM PROCESS

A. We understand that we may engage one or more neutral professional, such as a financial professional, a child specialist, a neutral facilitator/coach, and/or a mediator, trained in the Collaborative process. Either or both parties may also retain a Collaboratively-trained individual coach to work with him or her. We refer to these professionals, as well as our Collaborative attorneys, as "Collaborative professionals" in this document.

B. A neutral financial professional assists the participants with budgets, cash flow, and property division.

C. A neutral facilitator/coach may serve as a case manager and assists the participants in managing emotions, improving communication, developing coparenting skills, and establishing new boundaries and expectations.

D. A neutral child specialist meets with the children to understand their needs, provide a voice for the children, give feedback to the participants about their children's needs, and work with the participants to create a developmentally responsive parenting plan.

E. A mediator uses specialized skills in dispute resolution to help the participants reach an agreement.

F. An individual Coach is aligned with the client who retained the Coach and assists the client with communication and negotiation skills throughout the Collaborative case. If one client retains an aligned Coach, typically the other client does, as well, so that the clients and both Coaches can work on communication and negotiation skills in joint meetings as well as with the individual Participant.

G. When other Collaborative professionals are retained, the Participants will sign a Collaborative Process Participation Agreement with each professional.

H. Neither of us will unilaterally terminate a neutral Collaborative professional's engagement without first providing an opportunity for the team and both Participants to resolve any concern underlying the request for termination.

VIII. EXPERTS

A. We agree to use neutral experts for any issue that requires expert advice and/or recommendation. This does not prevent either Participant from using an expert to educate them on any issues in this matter, provided such use is disclosed to all Participants and professionals beforehand.

B. We will retain any neutral expert jointly, unless we agree otherwise in writing.

C. Any report, recommendation, or documents generated by, or any oral communication from, the neutral expert shall be shared with each of us and our respective attorneys and, unless otherwise agreed, covered by the confidentiality clause in Section XIV below.

IX. FEES AND COSTS

We recognize that we each have an obligation to our respective attorneys to pay their fees, and to pay the fees of our other retained Collaborative professionals. The source of funds used to satisfy our respective obligations is a matter to be addressed in the Collaborative process if so desired by either Participant. The fees for neutral Collaborative professionals shall be shared unless the Participants agree otherwise.

X. ENFORCEABILITY OF AGREEMENTS

A. **Temporary Agreements.** If either of us requires a temporary court order for any purpose, we will need to reach an agreement on the issues to be addressed by such an order, and then sign a written agreement. Such a temporary agreement is considered to be made pursuant to a commenced dissolution proceeding, and therefore, can be submitted to the court as the basis for an order, and enforced, if necessary.

We may also reach a temporary agreement on any matter and choose to ensure the enforceability of the agreement should the case not settle in this process, by including a provision in the agreement that it may be submitted to the court as a basis for a court order, and made retroactive to the date the written agreement was signed.

B. **Final Agreement.** Any final agreement we sign shall be submitted to the Court as the basis for entry of a Judgment and Decree of Dissolution.

XI. TERMINATION OF PROCESS PRIOR TO SETTLEMENT

A. **Termination of Process.** The Participants agree that participation in the Collaborative process is voluntary and that any Participant has the unilateral right to terminate the process, with or without cause, at any time. Termination of the Collaborative process occurs (1) when a Participant gives written notice to other Participant that the process is ended, or (2) when a Participant discharges a Collaborative attorney or a Collaborative attorney withdraws from further representation of a Participant, except as set forth in Section XI below.

B. **Withdrawal or Discharge of Collaborative Attorneys.** If an attorney-client relationship is terminated, and the Participant wishes to continue in the Collaborative process, the Participant shall provide prompt written notice of this intention to the team. Within 30 days of notice to the team of termination of a Collaborative attorney, the Participant shall retain a new Collaborative attorney, both Participants will sign a new Participation Agreement, and the Collaborative attorneys continuing on the case will acknowledge representation of the clients. If a new Agreement is not signed within the 30 day period, the other Participant shall be entitled to proceed as if the Collaborative process was terminated as of the date written notice of termination was given.

C. **Waiting Period.** Upon termination of the process, there will be a 30-day waiting period, absent an emergency, before the scheduling of any court hearing, to permit the Participants to retain new attorneys and make an orderly transition.

D. **Previous Agreements.** All written temporary agreements signed by the Participants shall remain in full force and effect until modified by agreement, or until issuance of a court order.

E. **No Surprise.** The intent of this section is to avoid surprise and prejudice to the rights of the non-withdrawing Participant.

F. **Presentation to Court.** We agree that either Participant may bring this provision to the attention of the Court in requesting the continuance of a hearing scheduled by the other or his/her attorney during the 30-day waiting period.

XII. DISQUALIFICATION

A. The Participants agree that a Collaborative attorney who represented a Participant under this Participation Agreement, or any attorney in a law firm with which a Collaborative attorney is associated, shall be disqualified from representing a Participant in a court or other proceeding related to the Collaborative matter(s) which is the subject of this Participation Agreement. After the signing of the Participation Agreement, neither Collaborative attorney may represent either Participant in any non-collaborative matter where the Participants have adverse interests.

B. Notwithstanding the Collaborative attorney disqualification provision, the Participants agree that a Collaborative attorney, or an attorney in a law firm with which the Collaborative attorney is associated, may represent a participant to request that a tribunal approve an agreement resulting from the Collaborative process, or to seek or defend an emergency order to protect the health, safety, welfare or interest of a Participant if a successor attorney is not immediately available to represent that person. However, once that Participant is represented by a successor attorney, or once reasonable measures have been taken to protect the health, safety, welfare or interest of that Participant, the Collaborative attorney disqualification provision applies.

XIII. ABUSE OF THE COLLABORATIVE PRACTICE PROCESS

A. The Participants agree that if either attorney learns of an abuse of the process, and the abuse cannot be remedied, the attorney who learns of the abuse must withdraw from the

case. Some examples of abuse of process include, but are not limited to:
- planning or threatening to flee the jurisdiction of the Court with our children;
- disposing of property without the consent of the other;
- withholding or misrepresenting relevant information; and
- failing to disclose the existence or true nature of assets, income or debts.

B. Attorneys will also consider withdrawing if either Participant, after coaching or consultation with their attorney or other Collaborative professionals, fails to participate reasonably in the Collaborative process.

XIV. CONFIDENTIALITY

A. **Communications in Court Proceedings.** All communication and information exchanged within the Collaborative process is confidential.

B. **Private Communications.** Just as in conventional legal practice, there will be private communications between each Participant and his or her respective attorney, and these communications are protected by the attorney-client privilege. Within the Collaborative process, however, we understand that open and honest communication is essential. We therefore understand that all information relevant to the issues we must decide, including that information which is attorney-client privileged, will normally be disclosed by our attorneys to team members, and we consent to such disclosure. We also understand, however, that we have the right to assert the attorney-client privilege at any time and may request that our attorneys not disclose information. We understand, however, that our failure to consent to disclosure of relevant information may result in termination of the process.

C. **Communications Between Collaborative Professionals.** For Collaborative professionals to work most efficiently and effectively together for the benefit of the Participants, Collaborative team professionals must be able to discuss relevant matters with one another. The Participants agree that Collaborative team professionals may communicate among themselves and that those communications may not necessarily be shared with the Participants.

D. **Communications Among All Collaborative Participants.** Sometimes it is most efficient for a Participant in the Collaborative process to communicate with both Collaborative attorneys and both clients, as well as any combination of other members of the Collaborative team or no other members of the Collaborative team, regarding matters such as scheduling, disbursement of meeting summaries and other information. By signing this Participation Agreement each Participant instructs his or her Collaborative attorney to permit communication between the Participant and the other Collaborative attorney provided that the Participant's own Collaborative attorney is copied on the communication, and each Collaborative attorney hereby does so permit.

E. **Disclosure of Receipt of Privileged Information.** If one Participant obtains privileged communications (electronic, voice and/or written communication between a participant and his or her attorney), he or she must disclose that fact to the other Participant and his or her own attorney. If one Participant copies or forwards privileged communication to a Collaborative professional, that Collaborative professional must disclose receipt of such privileged communication to the attorney involved in the communication, and destroy his or her copy.

F. **Confidentiality of Communications with Persons Outside the Collaborative Process.** All communication and information exchanged within the Collaborative process shall remain private and shall not be exchanged by the Participants or professionals with any other persons without the written agreement of both Participants. This provision does not prevent either Participant from disclosing such information as may be needed to obtain a second opinion from another attorney. Further, we understand that our lawyers are under an ethical obligation to report attorney misconduct. We understand that if our Collaborative case terminates prior to a settlement of all matters, our Collaborative attorneys will assist us in making an orderly transition by transferring our file to our new counsel. We understand that the file our attorneys will be providing to subsequent counsel consists of all documents we provided to our attorneys, and all written, signed agreements reached during the collaborative process. We agree that our file does not include the notes made during joint meetings by any of our collaborative professionals (see paragraph VII for definition of collaborative professionals), written communications between our collaborative professionals or the work product of any collaborative professionals except as provided in paragraph XIV, as these remain confidential. We understand that during the Collaborative process, minutes prepared at or after joint meetings will be provided to each of us, and we will receive copies of any parenting plan we create with our child specialist, any relationship plan created with our neutral facilitator/coach, and cash flow analyses and asset/liability sheets generated by our financial professional. We are each free to provide copies of these documents to subsequent litigation counsel, if we so choose, but understand that our lawyers and other team professionals will not be providing copies of these documents to subsequent counsel. Finally, by signing this Participation Agreement we are instructing our Collaborative attorneys not to talk about the substantive issues in our case, or any information related to the substantive issues learned in joint meetings or in team meetings between our Collaborative professionals, with our subsequent litigation counsel. This does not preclude our Collaborative attorneys from discussing procedural matters with subsequent counsel.

G. **Subsequent Litigation.** If subsequent litigation occurs, the Participants agree that:

(1) Neither Participant will introduce as evidence in court any written or oral information generated, or documents prepared, during the Collaborative process, including e-mails, voice mails, letters, progress notes, session notes, budgets and projections and proposals for settlement. Only documents such as sworn financial statements and original financial documents may be introduced in court, unless the Participants mutually agree otherwise; provided, however, that a Collaborative professional who generated a document cannot be compelled or subpoenaed to testify at any court hearing or deposition about matters related to the document.

(2) Neither Participant will introduce as evidence in court, nor require the production of, any reports, opinions or notes prepared by any other professional in the Collaborative process, except as follows: professional reports may be used in the event that the Collaborative process terminates on written consent of both Participants; provided, however, that the Collaborative professional who generated the report cannot be compelled or subpoenaed to testify at any court hearing or deposition about matters related to the report.

(3) Neither Participant will compel nor subpoena either Collaborative attorney or any other Collaborative professional retained in the Collaborative process to attend court or a deposition to testify about matters discussed in the Collaborative process. We intend this provision to benefit the Collaborative professionals on our case, and agree that Collaborative professionals shall be regarded as third party beneficiaries of this provision of our Participation Agreement, such that they can request enforcement of this contractual provision if any Participant seeks to compel or subpoena a professional to testify regarding matters discussed in the Collaborative process.

(4) Only the fact that Collaborative process was attempted and final settlement was not reached may be introduced into evidence in court, unless we agree otherwise in writing.

H. **Mandated Reporting of Child Abuse.** Notwithstanding the above, Collaborative Child Specialists and Coaches who are licensed mental health practitioners must report discovered child abuse to legal authorities pursuant to Minnesota statutory law.

XV. RIGHTS AND OBLIGATIONS PENDING SETTLEMENT

If we have signed a Joint Petition for the purpose of commencing a dissolution of marriage proceeding, we agree to be bound by the following notices as if a Summons had been served on each of us:

NOTICE OF TEMPORARY RESTRAINING PROVISIONS

UNDER MINNESOTA LAW, SERVICE OF THIS SUMMONS MAKES THE FOLLOWING REQUIREMENTS APPLY TO BOTH PARTICIPANTS TO THIS ACTION, UNLESS THEY ARE MODIFIED BY THE COURT OR THE PROCEEDING IS DISMISSED:

(1) NEITHER PARTICIPANT WILL DISPOSE OF ANY ASSETS EXCEPT (i) FOR THE NECESSITIES OF LIFE OR FOR THE NECESSARY GENERATION OF INCOME OR PRESERVATION OF ASSETS, (ii) BY AN AGREEMENT IN WRITING, OR (iii) TO RETAIN COUNSEL TO CARRY ON OR TO CONTEST THIS PROCEEDING;

(2) NEITHER PARTICIPANT MAY HARASS THE OTHER PARTICIPANT;

(3) ALL CURRENTLY AVAILABLE INSURANCE COVERAGE MUST BE MAINTAINED WITHOUT CHANGE IN COVERAGE OR BENEFICIARY DESIGNATION.
IF YOU VIOLATE ANY OF THESE PROVISIONS, YOU WILL BE SUBJECT TO SANCTIONS BY THE COURT.

XVI. ACKNOWLEDGMENTS

A. We acknowledge that we have read this Agreement, understand its terms and conditions, and agree to abide by them.

B. We understand that by agreeing to this alternative method of resolving our dissolution issues, we are giving up certain rights, including the right to formal discovery, formal court hearings, and other procedures provided by the adversarial legal system.

C. We have chosen the Collaborative process to reduce emotional and financial costs, and to generate a final agreement that addresses our concerns. We agree to work in good faith to achieve these goals.

XVII. PLEDGE

We hereby pledge to comply with and to promote the spirit and written word of this participation agreement.

_____ _____
DATED   DATED

_____ _____
FIRST M. LAST, PARTICIPANT   FIRST M. LAST, PARTICIPANT

ACKNOWLEDGEMENT OF REPRESENTATION

In the Collaborative process First M. Last will be represented by Attorney A. Name and First M. Last will be represented by Attorney B. Name.

_____ _____
DATED   DATED

_____ _____
FIRST M. LAST, PARTICIPANT   FIRST M. LAST, PARTICIPANT

I, Attorney A. Name, confirm that I will represent First M. Last in the Collaborative process and commit to the spirit of the Collaborative process expressed in this Participation Agreement.

_____
DATED

_____
ATTORNEY A. NAME, ATTORNEY

I, Attorney B. Name, confirm that I will represent First M. Last in the Collaborative process and commit to the spirit of the Collaborative process expressed in this Participation Agreement.

_____
DATED

_____
ATTORNEY B. NAME, ATTORNEY

Appendix B

Roadmap to Resolution

1. Understand and agree to the collaborative process

2. Identify goals and interests

3. Deal with interim issues
   - Temporary parenting issues (if any)
     - Sharing of time
     - Sharing of responsibilities
   - Temporary financial issues
     - Cash flow (expenses, income)
     - Status quo (spending limits, managing assets)
   - Temporary housing issues
   - Temporary use of personal property, furniture, furnishings, etc.

4. Gather facts relevant to the case
   - Decide what information is needed
   - Prepare initial lists of assets and liabilities
   - Provide and review certain financial information
   - Exchange and complete sworn inventories and appraisements
   - Review additional requested financial information
   - Review information to reach consensus and identify differences

5. Identify and evaluate options
   - Brainstorm—anything goes!

6. Negotiate, evaluate options, and reach agreement
   - Analyze the brainstorming options in the context of each party's interests
   - Evaluate the consequences of choosing the various possible resolutions
   - Eliminate ideas that do not sufficiently meet important goals of either party
   - Consider the possibility of combining options
   - Narrow the list of options down to those that most meet the interests of both parties
   - Finalize the agreement

Appendix C

Erik Erikson's Developmental Stages

STAGE	BASIC CONFLICT	IMPORTANT EVENTS	OUTCOME
Infancy (birth to 18 months)	Trust vs. Mistrust	Feeding	Children develop a sense of trust when caregivers provide reliability, care, and affection. A lack of this will lead to mistrust.
Early Childhood (2 to 3 years)	Autonomy vs. Shame and Doubt	Toilet Training	Children need to develop a sense of personal control over physical skills and a sense of independence. Success leads to feelings of autonomy, failure results in feelings of shame and doubt.
Preschool (3 to 5 years)	Initiative vs. Guilt	Exploration	Children need to begin asserting control and power over the environment. Success in this stage leads to a sense of purpose. Children who try to exert too much power experience disapproval, resulting in a sense of guilt.
School Age (6 to 11 years)	Industry vs. Inferiority	School	Children need to cope with new social and academic demands. Success leads to a sense of competence, while failure results in feelings of inferiority.
Adolescence (12 to 18 years)	Identity vs. Role Confusion	Social Relationships	Teens need to develop a sense of self and personal identity. Success leads to an ability to stay true to yourself, while failure leads to role confusion and a weak sense of self.

https://theoriesinpsychologyf10.wikispaces.com/Erikson's+Psychosocial+Stages+of+Development

For more information about developmental stages and parenting time, visit www.mncourts.gov/documents/0/Public/Court_Information_Office/Parenting_Time_Pamphlet.pdf.

Appendix D

Balance Sheet

DESCRIPTION	H W JT	MARITAL VALUE	NON-MARITAL VALUE	ALLOCATION OF VALUE HUSBAND	ALLOCATION OF VALUE WIFE	DATE OF VALUATION	SOURCE OF INFORMATION AND NOTES
Dated:							
Valuation Date:							
1) Real Estate:							
a)							
b)							
c)							
d)							
Subtotal		$	$	$	$		
2) Bank Accounts, Cash and Securities:							
a)							
b)							
c)							
d)							
Subtotal		$	$	$	$		
3) Retirement Accounts:							
a)							
b)							
c)							
d)							
Subtotal		$	$	$	$		

APPENDIX D

DESCRIPTION	H W JT	MARITAL VALUE	NON-MARITAL VALUE	ALLOCATION OF VALUE HUSBAND	WIFE	DATE OF VALUATION	SOURCE OF INFORMATION AND NOTES
4) Life Insurance:							
a)							
b)							
c)							
d)							
Subtotal		$	$	$	$		
5) Tax Refund:							
a)							
b)							
c)							
Subtotal		$	$	$	$		
6) Other Assets:							
a)							
b)							
c)							
d)							
Subtotal		$	$	$	$		
7) Liabilities:							
a)							
b)							
c)							
d)							
Subtotal		$	$	$	$		
Net Worth Allocation:		$	$	$	$		
Equalization:		$		$	$		

Appendix E

Cycle of Domestic Abuse

HONEYMOON

Victim's Response:
- sets up counseling for him
- drops legal proceedings
- agrees to return, stay, or take him back
- forgives
- hopeful
- relieved
- happy

Abuser:
- apologizes
- promises won't happen again • tries to justify his behavior
- blames drugs or alcohol
- declares love • wants to be intimate • buys gifts
- promises to get help
- promises to go to church • enlists family support • cries
- threatens suicide

TENSION BUILDING

Abuser:
- sensitive
- nitpicks • yelling
- withholds affection
- putdowns • threatens
- crazy-making behavior
- destroys property
- accusations of unfaithfulness
- isolates her
- engages her to argue

Victim's Response:
- attempts to calm
- tries to reason
- tries to satisfy with food
- agrees with
- avoidance
- withdraws
- compliant
- nurtures

DENIAL

ACUTE EXPLOSION

Abuser: verbally abuses & humiliates • slap • punch • kick • grab • forces sex • beats • prevents her from calling police or leaving • harasses & abuses children • restrains • spits • stalks • use of weapons • objects thrown

Victim's Response:
- protects self any way • tries to reason & calm
- may or may not call police • leaves • fights back

Adapted from Lenore Walker
The Battered Woman, 1979

Appendix F

Budget Form

EXPENSE	$
HOUSING	
Rent or Mortgage Payment	
Second Rent or Mortgage Payment	
Home Equity Loan Payment	
Contract for Deed Payment	
Real Estate Tax (if paid separately)	
Homeowner's/Renter's Insurance (if paid separately)	
Homeowner's Association Dues	
Major Home Repairs/Improvements	
Routine Home Repairs/Appliances	
Snow Removal	
Appliance Home Service/Repair Fees	
Carpet Cleaning	
Decorating	
Drain Service	
Furniture Cleaning	
Gardening & Landscaping	
Pool Maintenance	
House Cleaning	
House Painting	
Household Supplies	
Invisible Fence Repairs/Maintenance	
Lawn Mowing	

Spring/Fall Clean-up
Tree Trimming
Window Washing

Housing Subtotal

UTILITIES
Electricity
Gas/Heating Oil
Water/Sewer
Garbage/Trash
Internet
Home Telephone
Cell Phone
Telephone (long distance/other)
Cable TV
Water Softener
Alarm Monitoring
Utilities Subtotal
Food/Beverage
Groceries
Restaurant
Lunches at Work or School

Food/Beverage Subtotal

MEDICAL
Medical Insurance
Medical Bills (unreimbursed by Insurance)
Dental Insurance
Dental Bills (unreimbursed by Insurance)
Orthodontist
Medicines and Rx Drugs
Eyeglasses/Contacts
Counseling and Therapy
Health Club Membership
Medical Subtotal
Insurance General
Life Insurance
Short/Long-Term Disability Insurance

Accident

Health

Personal Property/Jewelry

Personal Umbrella

Other Insurance (specify)

Insurance Subtotal

TRANSPORTATION

Automobile Payments

Gas and Oil

Maintenance and Repairs (and cover insurance deductible)

Auto Insurance

License and Tabs

Parking

Car Wash

Motor Club Memberships (e.g., AAA, navigation system plans, etc.)

Vehicle Replacement Reserve

Other (airfare, bus fare, taxis, etc.)

Other Transportation Costs (specify)

Other Fuel Costs (specify)

Other Maintenance Costs (specify)

Other Insurance Costs (specify)

Other License Costs (specify)

Transportation Subtotal

EDUCATION

Books and Supplies

Community Education Classes

Computer/Computer Programs

Musical Instruments

Special Activities

Transportation/School Parking Pass

Tuition

Tutoring

Year Books/School Photos

Education Subtotal

CLOTHING/PERSONAL GROOMING

Clothing and Shoes

Laundry and Dry Cleaning	
Alterations and Repairs	
Grooming/Cosmetics/Personal	
Manicures/Pedicures	
Barber/Beautician	
Massage	
Clothing/Personal Grooming Subtotal	

CHILD CARE

Allowance	
Babysitter	
Birthday Parties	
Child Support	
Prior Child Support Obligations	
Day Care Center	
Preschool	
Diaper Service	
Lessons	
Parenting Consultant	
Religious School	
Summer/Day Camp	
Swimming Lessons	
Transportation	
Child Care Subtotal	

RECREATION/TRAVEL/ENTERTAINMENT

Concerts	
Country Club Dues	
Movies/Sporting Events	
Parties/Home Entertainment	
Season Tickets	
Vacations	
Recreation/Travel/Entertainment Subtotal	

MISCELLANEOUS

Costs of Employment	
Donations/Worship	
Gifts	
Hobbies	

Income Taxes (not withheld)	
Prior Spousal Maintenance Obligation	
Memberships/Clubs	
Papers/Books/Magazines	
Pet Grooming/License	
Veterinary	
Postage	
Retirement/IRA Fees	
Savings—Pension Contributions (est.)	
Spending Money	
Visitation Expenses	
Other (specify)	
Miscellaneous Subtotal	
SUBTOTAL EXPENSES	$
TOTAL EXPENSES	$

Notes

Chapter 1

1. The Gottman Institute, http://www.gottman.com.
2. John Gottman and Nan Silver, "What Makes Marriage Work?" *Psychology Today*, March 1, 1994 (last reviewed on June 19, 2012).
3. Ibid.

Chapter 5

1. Colleen O'Connor, "New Law Changes Alimony Landscape for Divorcing Colorado Couples," *The Denver Post*, October 18, 2013.

Chapter 6

1. Toni Bernhard, "Four Tips for Slowing Down to Reduce Stress," *Psychology Today*, September 13, 2011.
2. R. A. Emmons, et al., "Counting Blessings versus Burdens: An Experimental Investigation of Gratitude and Subjective Well-Being in Daily Life," *Journal of Personality and Social Psychology* Vol. 84, No. 2, (Feb. 2003): 377–89.
3. M. E. P. Seligman, et al., "Empirical Validation of Interventions," *American Psychologist* Vol. 60, No. 1, (July–Aug. 2005): 410–21.
4. Alex M. Wood, et al., "The Role of Gratitude in the Development of Social Support, Stress, and Depression: Two Longitudinal Studies," *Journal of Research in Personality*, Volume 42, No. 4 (2008): 854—871.
5. Sara Algoe, et al. "Beyond Reciprocity: Gratitude and Relationships in Everyday Life," *Emotion* Vol. 8, No. 3, June 2008: 425–429.

6. Amie Gordon, PhD, "Gratitude Is for Lovers," February 5, 2013. (Retrieved January 10, 2015, from http://greatergood.berkeley.edu/article/item/gratitude_is_for_lovers)

7. Elisabeth Kübler-Ross, *The Final Stage of Growth* (New York: Touchstone, 1975), 96.

8. Elisabeth Kübler-Ross, *On Death and Dying: What the Dying Have to Teach Doctors, Nurses, Clergy & Their Own Families* (New York: Scribner, 1969).

9. American Bar Association: Commission on Domestic & Sexual Violence, "Survey of Recent Statistics," May 26, 2015, http://www.americanbar.org/groups/domestic_violence/resources/statistics.html.

Chapter 9

1. "The Stages of Life," in *Collected Works of C.G. Jung, Volume 8: Structure & Dynamics of the Psyche*, Gerhard Adler and R. F. C. Hull, eds. and trans. (Princeton: Princeton University Press, 1970), 784.

2. Debbie Ford, *Spiritual Divorce: Divorce as a Catalyst for an Extraordinary Life* (New York: HarperCollins, 2001).

3. Ibid, 83.

4. Ibid, 81.

5. Dr. Fred Luskin, *Forgive for Good: A Proven Prescription for Health and Happiness* (New York: HarperCollins, 2002) 78–79.

6. Ibid, 201.

7. Ibid, 110.

8. Ibid, 119–120.

9. Ibid, 203.

10. Greg S. Reid, Master Storyteller, http://bookgreg.com.

11. Dr. Gail Matthews, "Goals Research Summary," May 26, 2015, http://www.dominican.edu/academics/ahss/undergraduate-programs-1/psych/faculty/fulltime/gailmatthews/researchsummary2.pdf

12. Amir Levine, MD and Rachel S. F. Heller, MA *Attached: The New Science of Adult Attachment and How It Can Help You Find—and Keep—Love* (New York: Jeremy P. Tarcher/Penguin, 2010).

13. Gary D. Chapman, *The 5 Love Languages: The Secret to Love That Lasts* (Chicago, Northfield Publishing, 1992).

14. Kenneth Blanchard, Cynthia Olmstead, and Marcia Lawrence, *Trust Works! Four Keys to Building Lasting Relationships* (New York: HarperCollins, 2013).

References

Blanchard, K. and Olmstead, C. *Trust works! Four Keys to Building Lasting Relationships*. New York: William Morrow, 2013.

Chapman, G. *The 5 Love Languages: The secret to Love That Lasts*. Chicago: Northfield Pub, 2010.

Cohen, L. *Let Us Compare Mythologies*. Toronto: McClelland and Stewart, 1966.

Ford, D. *Spiritual Divorce: Divorce as a Catalyst for an Extraordinary Life*. San Francisco: HarperSanFrancisco, 2001.

Gottman, J. and Silver, N. *Why Marriages Succeed or Fail and How You Can Make Yours Last*. New York: Simon & Schuster, 2012.

Hanson, R. and Mendius, R. *Buddha's Brain: The Practical Neuroscience of Happiness, Love, and Wisdom*. Oakland, CA: New Harbinger Publications, 2009.

Jung, C. Modern Man in Search of a Soul. New York: Harcourt, Brace & World, 1933.

Kübler-Ross, E. *On Death and Dying*. New York: Macmillan, 1969.

————. *Death: The Final Stage of Growth*. Englewood Cliffs, N.J.: Prentice-Hall, 1975.

Levine, A. and Heller, R. *Attached: The New Science of Adult Attachment and How It Can Help You Find—and Keep—Love*. New York: Jeremy P. Tarcher, 2010.

Luskin, F. *Forgive for Good: A Proven Prescription for Health and Happiness*. San Francisco: HarperSanFrancisco, 2002.

Smith, R. *Lies at the Altar: The Truth About Great Marriages*. New York: Hyperion, 2006.

Wallerstein, J. and Blakeslee, S. *What About the Kids? Raising Your Children Before, During, and After Divorce*. New York: Hyperion, 2003.

Suzanne GRANDCHAMP

author • speaker • attorney • coach

Connect with Suzanne Grandchamp or
order additional copies of this book online at:

Web/Blog: suzannegrandchamp.com
Facebook: facebook.com/sgrandchamp
Email: info@suzannegrandchamp.com

CPSIA information can be obtained
at www.ICGtesting.com
Printed in the USA
BVOW08s1713230318
511305BV00003B/292/P